IN NO TIME

Access
97

In No Time

Access 97

Ignatz Schels

Edited by
Rob Young

Prentice Hall Europe

London New York Toronto Sydney Tokyo Singapore Madrid Mexico City Munich Paris

First published in 1997 as Easy – Access 97 by
Markt&Technik Buch- und Software Verlag GmbH
85540 Haar bei München/Germany
This edition published 1999 by
Prentice Hall Europe
Campus 400, Maylands Avenue
Hemel Hempstead
Hertfordshire, HP2 7EZ

A division of
Simon & Schuster International Group

Translated by Karen Green, Elaine Richman and Martin James
in association with First Edition Translations Limited, Cambridge

Typeset in Stone Sans
by Clare Oliver

Designed and Produced by Bender Richardson White

Printed and bound in Great Britain
by TJ International, Padstow, Cornwall

Library of Congress Cataloging-in-Publication Data

Available from the publisher

British Library Cataloguing in Publication Data

A catalogue record for this book is available from the British Library

ISBN 0-13-977646-X

1   2   3   4   5   02   01   00   99   98

Contents

2 Office management workshop 44

3 Address management 78

4 Your personal music collection 114

Dear readers,

So you want to learn how to use the database program Access 97. I'm pleased that you've decided to use my book for this, and I'm sure it's a decision you won't regret.

In all my years running seminars on this kind of software, my experience has always been the same: software is written by programmers, and they often seem to think that users need to know as much as they do. Which is why the screen masks, the manuals and the help texts are often so difficult to follow.

But I'd like to show you it doesn't have to be this way. You will find you are being taught the essentials of the software in an easy-to-understand way, with the links being shown where necessary, terms explained easily and the step-by-step instructions given to help you get results and succeed fast.

So what do I expect of you? You need to be familiar with the Windows operating system to some extent. Otherwise, all you need is to enjoy what you do, be curious and want to get things done. And, of course, a little patience coupled with a sense of humour if everything doesn't go quite as smoothly as it should. So there's really very little to stop you using Access 97 successfully.

So have fun – and good luck with your software and 'Access 97 In No Time'.

The author

Ignatz Schels

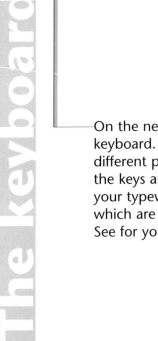

The keyboard

On the next three pages, we'll look at the keyboard. To keep things simple, we'll show you different parts of the keyboard in turn. Many of the keys are exactly the same as the ones on your typewriter; but there are some other keys which are needed for using the computer. See for yourself …

Typewriter keys

You use these keys in just the same way as on your typewriter, and use the Enter key to send commands to the computer.

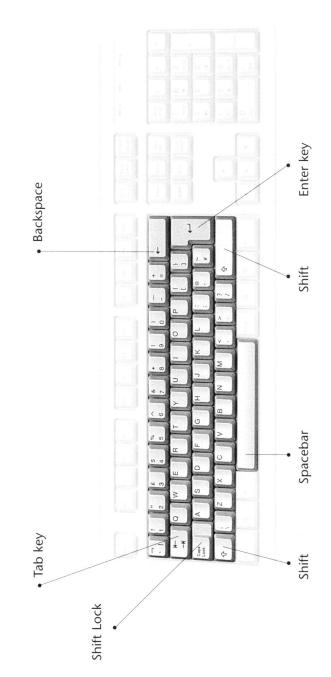

Tab key

Shift Lock

Backspace

Enter key

Shift

Spacebar

Shift

Special keys, function keys, indicator lights, numerical keypad

The special keys and the function keys are used specially for working with the computer. The Ctrl, Alt and Alt Gr keys are normally used in combination with other keys. The Esc key is used to cancel commands, and Insert and Delete to insert and delete text.

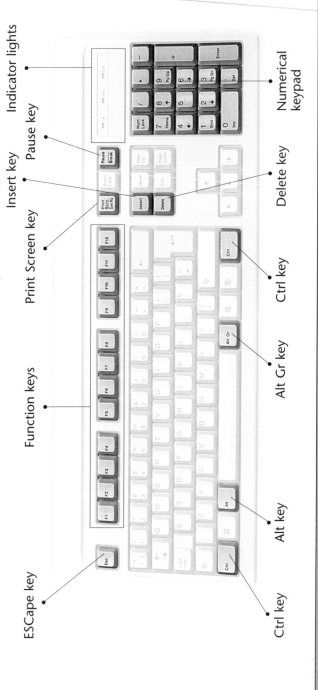

ESCape key

Function keys

Print Screen key

Insert key Pause key

Indicator lights

Ctrl key Alt key Alt Gr key Ctrl key

Delete key

Numerical keypad

Cursor keys

These keys are used for moving the cursor around on the screen.

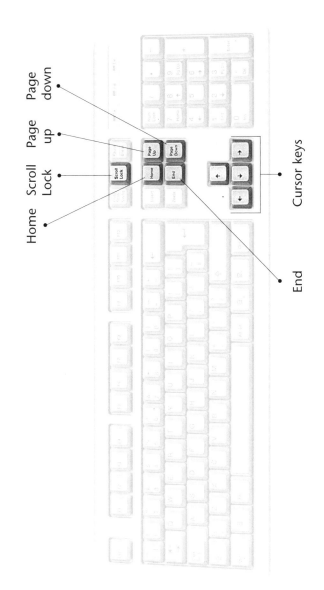

Home · Scroll Lock · Page up · Page down · End · Cursor keys

13

'Clicking'
means pressing a
key quickly once.

Click the left-hand
mouse key

Click the right-hand
mouse key

'Double-clicking' means clicking the
left-hand mouse key twice in quick
succession

Double-click

'Dragging and dropping'
With some elements on screen, you
can click the left-hand mouse key
and hold it down, move the mouse
and move the element to another
position.

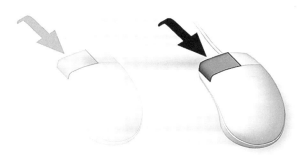

Dragging and dropping

15

Databases – the basics

What's in this chapter?

What is a database? How is a database made and opened, and what's in it? In this chapter, you'll find the answers to these and other questions about databases. You will discover how to use a database which has already been set up, and learn to use Access to set up databases of your own. So let's start by taking a look at a typical professional database, the modules and how they link together.

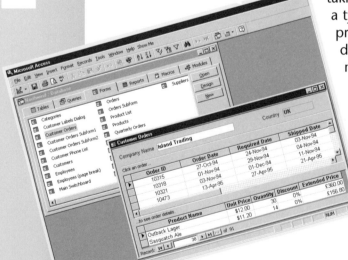

You are going to learn:

17

The basics

Before you start using Access, there are some basic terms used in connection with databases that you need to know. First, let's look at what a database and a database management system actually mean:

A **database** is a collection of data, consisting of tables, forms, queries and reports; bigger databases also have macros and modules.

A **database management system (DBMS)** is used for recording, saving, updating and managing a database. Access is a DBMS, and can be used to set up new databases and manage existing ones.

A **table** breaks down into data 'fields' and 'records'. The fields are the columns in the table, the records the rows. Each field has a field name.

Tables are the heart of a database. This is where data is held. Using the database management system, you can enter data in tables and link data from different tables to form a relational system.

Here is a little table with five fields and three records. The top line of a table always contains the field names:

First name	Surname	Street	Town	Postcode
Graham	Bond	Finch Street	Brighton	BN1 3NU
Peter	Berger	Milton Road	Coventry	CV3 5JD
Albert	Judge	Port Road	Liverpool	L11 4RE

A **field characteristic** lays down rules on the contents of the field: these must be followed when entering data in the table.

To prevent just any old data being input to the table, we can use the DBMS to include so-called field characteristics. One of the characteristics of the 'Name' field, for instance, could be the field length (e.g. more than 0 characters, not more than 20). You also need to specify how you want the 'Postcode' field set up, so that you can enter a maximum of six characters, ending with a number and two letters.

In **relational** databases, there are links between different tables. This lets you search for data in different files if that data has a common code.

Access databases are relational, which means that the tables are related to one another. When designing a database, it is essential to get these links set up properly right at the start. The better the links, the simpler you'll find it to analyse data later on.

Take a simple example: let's assume you want to set up a product database. The table might look like this:

Product code	Product name	Price	Manufacturer
1001	Screwdriver	2.99	Johnson Ltd
1002	Spirit level	12.95	KT Tools
etc			

Then you'll need a second table to hold all the manufacturers' details:

Manufacturer code	Manufacturer	Location	Tel. no
1001	Johnson Ltd	Manchester	0161 462 5524
1002	KT Tools	London	0181 542 8993

But setting it up like this could cause problems. Supposing you start using a different manufacturer? How can you find the products for all the manufacturers from a given area? Before you even start thinking about setting up a database, you need to think about what you want out of it, and the best way of doing this is to set up a relationship between the two tables. Let's set up Table 1 differently: instead of the manufacturer, we'll just save their number:

Product code	Product name	Price	Manufacturer code
1001	Screwdriver	2.99	1001
1002	Spirit level	12.95	1002

Next create a relationship between the two tables, and with a series of questions, you can pick out specific information from the tables.

Product name	Manufacturer
Screwdriver	1001
Spirit level	1001

relationship

Manufacturer code	Manufacturer	Location
1001	Johnson Ltd	Manchester
1002	KT Tools	London

Product name	Manufacturer	Location
Screwdriver	Johnson Ltd	Manchester
Spirit level	KT Tools	London

Starting Access

But that's enough theory. Let's start the program, so you can begin to use this book to find out about databases.

The **Microsoft Office 97** package consists of Word, Excel, PowerPoint and Outlook. The Professional version also includes Access.

Access is already installed on your hard disk (at least, we assume it is). If you still have it only on CD-ROM (in the Professional Office package), you'll have to load it onto your hard disk using the installation software.

When you switch on your computer, you may find the system will ask for your password and user name, if the computer you're using is on a network.

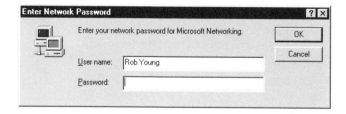

Once you've entered these, the desktop will appear. From this desktop, you can select symbols to boot software.

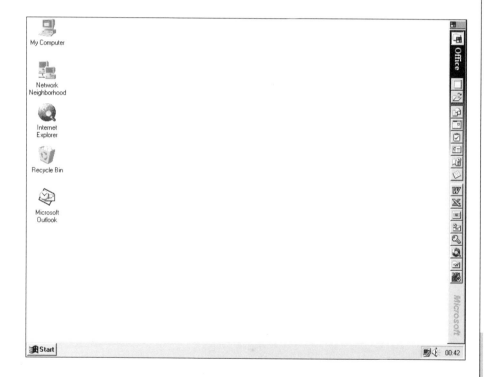

On the far right-hand side of the screen, you'll see the 'Shortcut' bar. To boot a program, all you have to do is click on the appropriate symbol in this bar.

A **task** means software which is running, i.e. is in RAM.

At the foot of the screen is the task bar. This is a bar in which all the software currently running leaves a little box. Just click the mouse on the box to switch to that task. Or you can click on the Start menu on the left-hand side.

The next thing you need to learn is how to start Access (and close it again):.

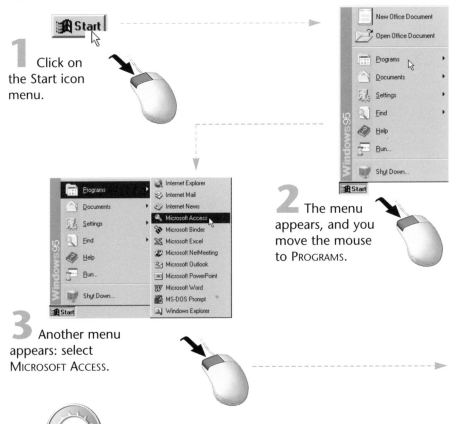

1 Click on the Start icon menu.

2 The menu appears, and you move the mouse to PROGRAMS.

3 Another menu appears: select MICROSOFT ACCESS.

4 The system runs Access, the program appears on the desktop and a dialog field appears. Click on *Cancel* to close it.

5 Now all you can see is the program window and header bar, the menu bar and toolbar.

6 Open the FILE menu ...

23

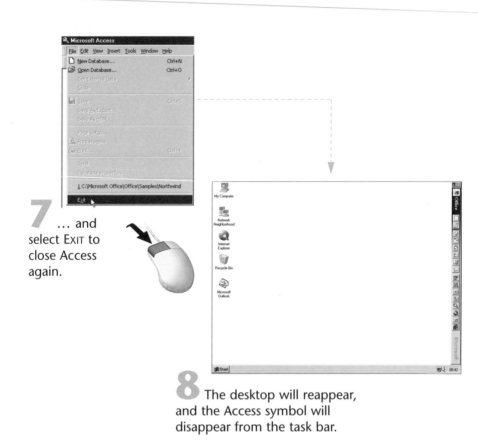

7 ... and select EXIT to close Access again.

8 The desktop will reappear, and the Access symbol will disappear from the task bar.

Finding your way around in folders and drives

Of course, when you enter data into your computer, you don't just keep filling it up until it's full. Your computer – or, more accurately, your computer's hard drive, is divided into folders, and we need to take a good look at this folder structure before we start using our database software to generate and save data.

There are some basic definitions which you should be familiar with:

A **drive** is a data medium which is used to hold data. In practice, this is almost always a hard disk. If you're on a network, the drive you want may be on another computer altogether. Drives are listed from A to Z: the hard drive is usually the C drive.

A drive is divided into **folders**. The main folder at the topmost level contains subfolders and also files. In many cases, the path, that is, the way to a folder, is shown by listing the individual folders involved in the order in which they occur, separated by backslashes:
C:\Software\Myfiles

Anything which is saved on a data medium must be held as a **file**. These files are known by their filename and an extension. The filename can be up to 255 characters long, the extension is three characters. Any folder in the tree can hold as many files as you like.

The best way to get to know your way around the drives, directories and files is to use Windows Explorer. This is a part of the Windows package which you can use not only to display files, but also to copy, move and delete them. (You will need this if your hard disk ever gets so full there is no room for any more files!)

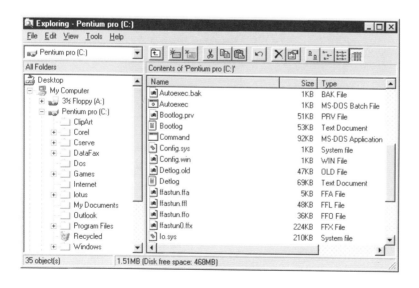

How does Access set up databases on the hard disk? Here, the manufacturers had a bright idea: everything you can get into a database is held in just a single file. The file extension is **MDB**, for **M**icrosoft **D**ata**b**ase. This database file can hold up to 1 Gigabyte (= 1000 Mb) of data. But, if that's not enough, you can add on more files, so your database can be more or less any size you like.

And where do you save databases on a hard disk? That's something you can decide yourself. Access doesn't tell you what drive to put the database on or in what folder. But the best way (and not just for Access!) is always to keep a specific folder for the files that a given program generates. It makes your data easier to find again, and if you have to copy or move anything from one database to another, you can do this faster if the files are close to one another.

Which folder holds your database files, is easy to find. Just as easily, you could set up another folder and declare it as your *default database directory*. In the exercises in this book, we'll set up a new folder called *Access easy* and set Access up so it retrieves and saves all data to and from this new folder.

1 From the Windows Start menu, start Windows Explorer.

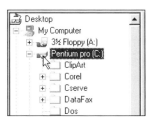

2 Select the first level of the folder structure by clicking on the icon for the hard disk drive (although it almost certainly won't be called 'Pentium Pro' on your computer).

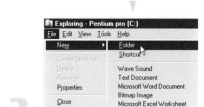

3 Use this menu option to set up a new folder.

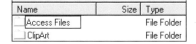

4 Enter the name you want to call the folder and then press .

5 Now you can start Access from the Start menu or via the shortcut bar.

27

6 When you start Access, a dialog field will appear. Select *New database*.

7 The first thing you have to do is give the database a name. Access then adds this name to the default database directory.

8 When you open this list, you'll see what level in the directory structure this directory is on.

9 Click on the drive symbol to go back to root level.

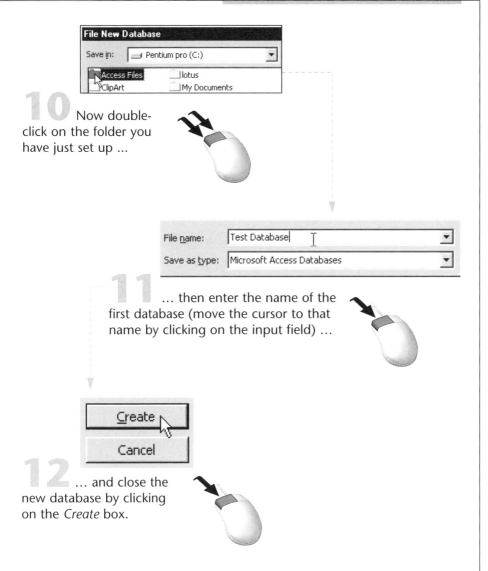

10 Now double-click on the folder you have just set up ...

11 ... then enter the name of the first database (move the cursor to that name by clicking on the input field) ...

12 ... and close the new database by clicking on the *Create* box.

As long as you are still using Access, this folder will be your working folder. Any time you want to open a database, this is where the system will look, and this is where it will save the new database you have just set up.

To make sure your database data always ends up in this directory, you need to specify it as your *default database* directory.

1 A database is active. Open the TOOLS menu ...

2 ... and select OPTIONS.

3 A dialog will appear, with ten tabbed pages. Using the mouse, click on the *General* tab.

Default Database Folder:

C:\My Documents

4 This input field shows the path which leads
to the directory containing the Access data.
Move the cursor to the field.

Default Database Folder:

C:\Access Files

5 Drag the mouse
across all the letters to
highlight them and type
your directory name to
replace them.

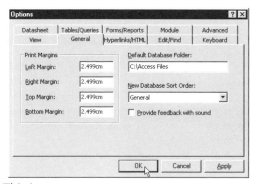

6 This is now
your new default
database directory.
Press OK to confirm.

Now close Access again straight away, select END from the FILE menu
and reboot the program again to check the new settings. If you
select the first option, to set up a new blank database or the default
option *Open an Existing Database*, you will automatically see the
contents of your default database directory.

31

A typical database: Northwind

Designing databases isn't easy. If you have to use databases for work or private purposes, you will need to put in a lot of time on the subject learning theory before you can get started. Of course, as the people who wrote Access, Microsoft are familiar with these problems and have done everything they can to make things easy for users.

How do you build a database? The best way of answering this is to look at a typical professional database – and one of these comes as part of the Access package. The *Northwind.mdb* database is a typical example, which shows you the main points of using a database.

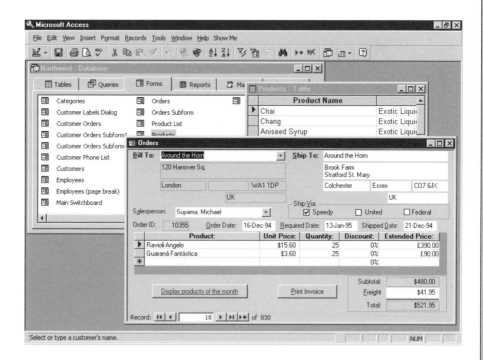

Our make-believe company, Northwind Traders, imports and exports fine foods from all over the world. Its database manages:

➡ The company's product data

➡ A register of all suppliers, including addresses, telephone numbers and Internet addresses

➡ Names and addresses of sales staff, with details of their training and photos of them

➡ A list of agents who can be used for importing/exporting

➡ The orders received for the products, with order dates, dispatch view and freight costs.

So let's have a look at this typical database. When Access was set up on our theoretical computer, it was put in the Office\Samples folder:

Start Access. In the first dialog field, select *Open an Existing Database*, or if the program window is already open, use the menu command FILE/OPEN DATABASE.

33

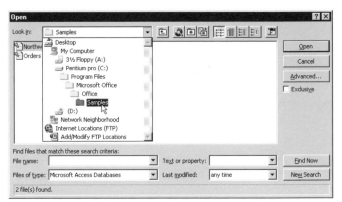

2 On your hard disk, look for the folder
Program Files\Microsoft Office\Office\Samples.

3 Open the
database
Northwind.mdb by
double-clicking on
the filename.

4 The database is opened, and
an introductory message appears
reminding you that this is a
sample application.

5 Click on this option so this
message doesn't appear every
time you open the database.

6 The first and most important thing you see in the database is the database window. This shows everything that's in the database. Double-click on the first table ...

7 ... and you'll see the records it contains. To close the table again, click on the cross symbol in the header bar in the top right-hand corner of the window.

8 Look at the forms. Click on the *Forms* tab, ...

35

9 ... and open the form for managing the product table you saw just now.

10 And these are the enquiries requesting records from one or more tables and outputting them in table form.

11 Use reports to prepare records for printing. A report is always based on a table or query.

12 This is the *Alphabetical List of Products* in page view. To close it, click on the X box again.

You'll find some more entries in the *Macros* section. This holds macros, in other words, little programs within programs. A macro contains a series of instructions which are executed when you run that macro (e.g. open a form, enter a date, produce a report etc.).

The final module, called *Modules,* is reserved for real programs, which are written in the programming language Visual Basic for Applications (or VBA). VBA programs run professional databases, hold dialogs with users and provide a lot of facilities for importing/ exporting data and working with the operating system. VBA is also called a development environment.

Relationships are what matter

As in real life, in a big database, relationships are what matter. As you saw in 'Basics' above, the individual tables in a database must be related to one another if they have to deal with one another. For instance, the product table is connected to the supplier table, because the first table only holds the supplier's number, while the second contains all the other data about that supplier.

In the Relationships window, you can check what relationships there are between the different tables and even create relationships between tables yourself if need be.

1 Open the TOOLS menu and select RELATIONSHIPS.

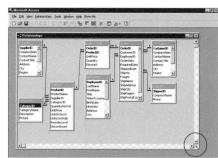

2 Enlarge the window by clicking the left-hand mouse key on the lower right-hand corner, holding the mouse key down and pulling out the window frame to the size you want.

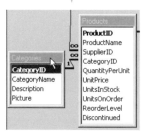

3 To move the *Categories* table, highlight the name and drag and drop the window with the mouse.

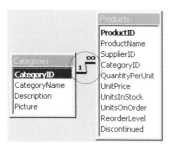

4 The line between the windows shows what kind of link this is – in this case between the categories table and products.

5 Double-clicking on the line opens a window which explains the link in detail.

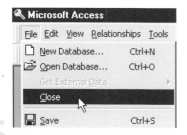

6 Now close the link window again via the FILE menu.

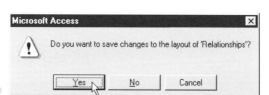

7 When you see this message, answer *Yes*. It just reminds you that the layout of windows and lines has been changed.

39

Design view and datasheet

There are two ways of using anything in a database, whether it be a table, a form or a report. You can either design it, change it and redesign it, or you can use it and record data or print records out on a printer. Access supports this strict job separation by showing the object either in **Design** view or as a **Datasheet/Form**.

If you want to add another column to a table, for instance, you can certainly open the object in design view. But to add a new customer to the customer table, you must open it in datasheet view. If the address on a form is too low down, you will need to use design view to change it. To display or edit the records one field at a time, you'll need to switch to form or datasheet view.

Let's have a look at these views and switching between them using our example database, Northwind.mdb and the customer data table:

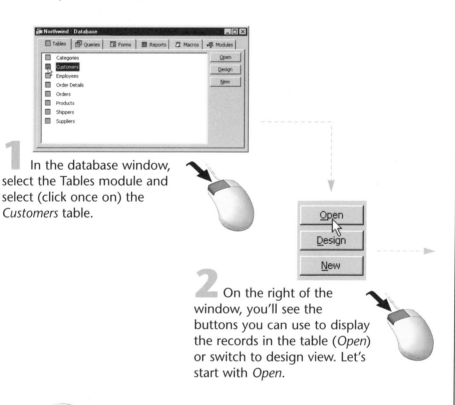

1 In the database window, select the Tables module and select (click once on) the *Customers* table.

2 On the right of the window, you'll see the buttons you can use to display the records in the table (*Open*) or switch to design view. Let's start with *Open*.

3 The table is opened, and the records appear. In the lower left-hand corner, you can see what record is being displayed and how many records the table contains. Now close the table again by clicking on the *Close* symbol.

4 Now for Design view. Click on the appropriate box, ...

5 ... and you'll see the structure of the table. Each column contains a field, which in turn contains a field name, a field data type and a field description.

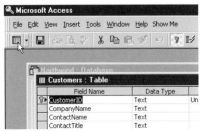

6 In the top left-hand corner of the symbol bar, you'll find a symbol which you can use to switch straight from one view to another. It always shows the next view, in this case Datasheet, ...

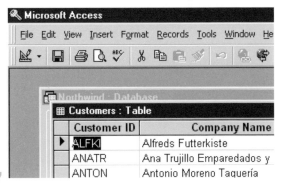

7 ... and click again to return to design view.

8 If you click on the little black triangle next to the symbol, you'll see the different views available.

Quick progress check

In this chapter, you've learnt some of the important basics about databases and had a look at a professionally designed Access database. Can you remember all the terms which were used? This little fill-in-the-gaps exercise below will help you memorise them.

DBMS stands for —————— (1). It means the software used to manage a database.

Databases consist of —————— (2), forms, —————— (3), reports, macros and modules.

The heart of a database is tables that are linked together. A database with links is called a —————(4)——

Each column in a table is called a —————— (5). The column heading is also the field name. To predefine the field size or contents, you will need to change the —————— (6).

You can start Access via the —————— (7) or shortcut bar.

An Access database is saved in a file with the extension —————— (8). The file can be up to —————— (9) in size.

To set the default database directory, use the menu command —————— (10).

The example database *Northwind.mdb* has tables which are linked to one another; to see the links, use the menu command —————— (11).

The database window contains —————— (12) modules. You can use the —————— (13) box to view an object (such as a table) in design view. In the top left-hand corner of the symbol bar, you'll find a symbol which you can use to switch the table to —————— (14).

You'll find the answers in the appendix.

Office management workshop

What's in this chapter?

In this workshop, you'll be looking at the most important part of a database – the table. Once you have worked through this chapter, you should know what a table structure is, and be familiar with the terms 'table field' and 'record'. You'll also learn how to input data, scroll through tables and sort them by individual fields. By then, you should be able to design all kinds of tables and enter data.

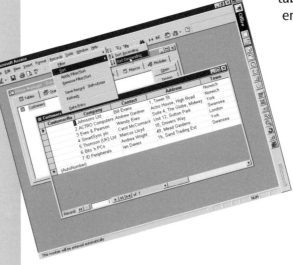

You already know:

You are going to learn:

In this workshop, you will set up a new database and add some tables. As you already know from the previous chapter, everything Access has to offer is based on tables. So, when you're designing a database, the first thing you need to think about is what tables will be in it.

Take office administration, for example. If you're an assistant or secretary, you will always be dealing with a wide range of data. However, if you're using Access for yourself, there won't be so much data but you'll find that even your own private database can contain a whole load of tables. Let's draw up a list of the tables your database might contain:

Customers

No office would be the same without them: for standard letters, address labels, telephone numbers and addresses, for analysing contacts, sales analyses, order frequency etc. As well as a full address and telephone and email numbers, don't forget to add the name of the person to speak to, and a 'comments' field is often a good idea too (hobbies, ideas for possible gifts).

Products

The products the company sells, the product base, product range and quantities in stock, unit prices, cost and selling price. Not forgetting the packaging units (litres, kilograms, by the box etc.) for special analysis. EANs (European Article Numbers) are often used as the key field.

Private collections

Your CD collection with titles, artists, type of music, number of tracks and assessment criteria; your recipe database; your electronic wine cellar and much more.

Training and education

Teachers can keep their pupil files, lesson and seminar details, and link it all to a course management system. Sports trainers can use Access to plan tournaments, competitions and fixtures.

The important thing is to use databases for the purpose for which they were designed. Don't try to manage data that would be better off under another software package. If you want to plan your appointments, for instance, you'd be better off using Outlook; and Excel is better for calculating your depreciation. Access is primarily a 'data grab': what it does best is saving and analysing data in large quantities.

A new table

Your first table will contain the addresses of your business contacts and customers. Every business uses customer details, whatever its size. Even private users find an address book very helpful, provided they keep it up to date, of course.

Start Access from the Start menu.

Select the first option, *Blank Database* to set up a new database

3 Click to confirm the option.

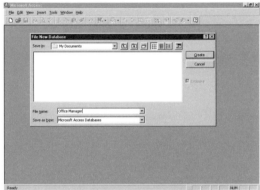

4 As the new database will not just be holding addresses, we will call the whole thing *Office Manager*. Enter the name (with no extension), …

5 … and click on *Open* to confirm.

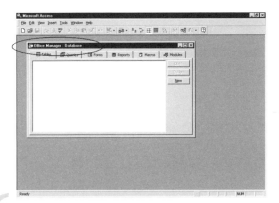

6 The system creates the database and saves it at the same time. You can see the title in the database window.

7 The first module, *Tables*, is still blank, so only the *New* button is available. Click on this, ...

8 ...and select Design View for the new table, ...

49

9 … and click on OK to confirm.

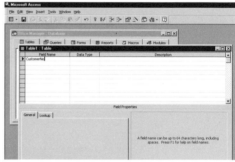

10 Now you'll see the table design window. Enter the first fieldname.

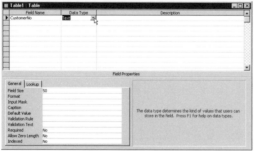

11 Press the ⏎ key to go to the next column. Here, you will open a list of field data types.

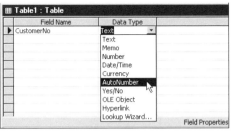

12 Your customers should be numbered in sequence, which is where the *AutoNumber* field type comes in.

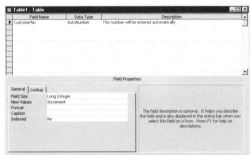

13 Press the ⏎ key again to go to the next column and enter the description of this field. Press ⏎ again to move onto the next line.

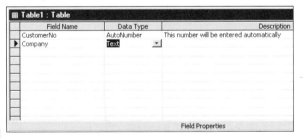

14 You can now set up the first text field for the company names. Press ⏎ to confirm the field data type.

15 After the description, you can add a field for the contact name. The more fields you use, the better you will be able to analyse the data later.

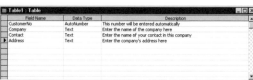

16 Another line is reserved for the road, ...

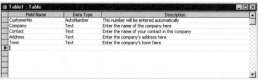

17 ... and the postcode field is also of this type.

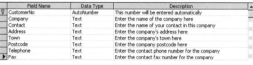

18 Which just leaves the town (text field) and customer's telephone number. Use one field each for the phone and fax numbers.

So that's our list of fields for the new table complete, for the moment at least. Check again to make sure you've entered all the fieldnames correctly.

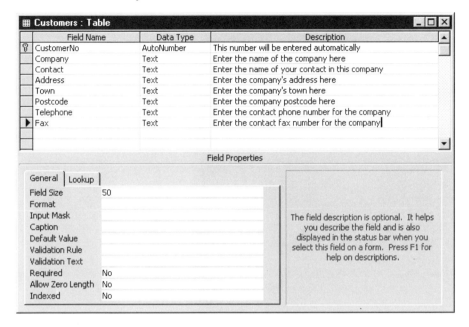

The fieldname rules to remember are as follows:

Allowed	Not allowed
Up to 64 letters and numbers. Names should begin with a letter. Special characters such as space, dash and dollar sign ($) are allowed, but are best avoided.	Full stop (.), exclamation mark (!), accents (' `) and square brackets ([ ]).

Don't forget the bottom half of the design window, which shows the characteristics of the field you're working on at present. The field size for text fields, for instance, is always 50 (characters), although of course you can vary this to suit individual fields.

Saving a table design

You have finished designing your first table. Now you can save it. Which brings us to a new definition – the primary key.

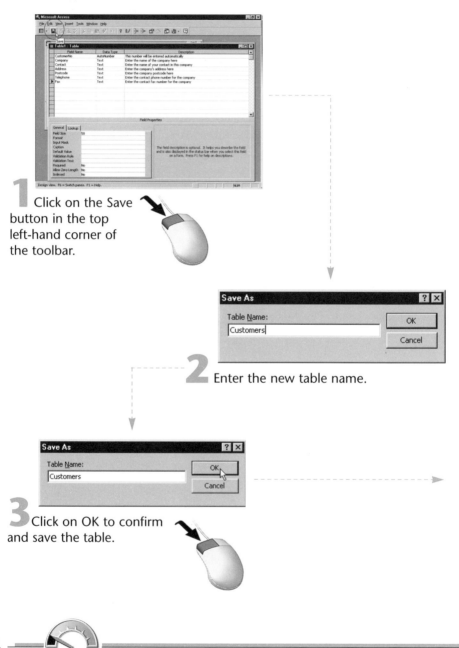

1 Click on the Save button in the top left-hand corner of the toolbar.

2 Enter the new table name.

3 Click on OK to confirm and save the table.

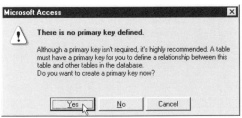

At this point, the
Office Assistant (or, if you
switched it off, this
message field from
Access) will appear and
suggest the primary key.
Click on *Yes* to confirm.

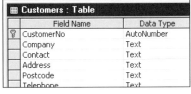

The first field in the table shows
the primary key (you can see it to the
left of the icon).

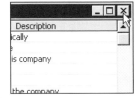

The table has
now been saved,
and you can close
the design window.

And this is the database window
with the first entry in the tables
module. Clicking on the *Design* button
will take you straight back to the list of
fields for that table.

55

WHAT'S THIS?

So what is a **primary key**? With Access, this means a field in the table which is unique. In this case, for example, it is the customer number, which is numbered consecutively using an *AutoNumber* field (no two customer numbers are the same). Access needs this primary key to establish links between tables. Primary keys come in a number of kinds, but the unique key we are using here is the commonest.

Entering data in the table

Your first table is now ready for you to put data into it. You learned how to do this in the chapter on 'basics'. You go to datasheet view to display the data in the table, enter data field by field, amend it or delete it. Design view was the view you used to establish the structure of the table, with field names, field data types and descriptions.

You can now start entering your customer data. You can always open tables in the table module by using the *Open* button, but double-clicking the table's icon is faster.

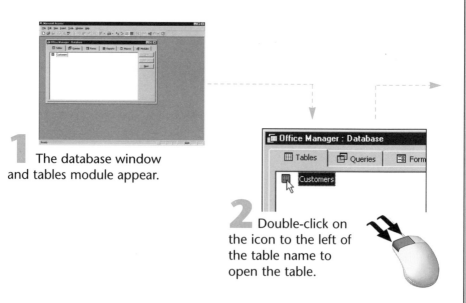

1 The database window and tables module appear.

2 Double-click on the icon to the left of the table name to open the table.

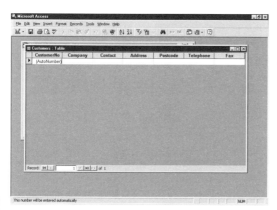

3 The table is now ready for data to be input. You'll see the cursor flashing in the first field of the first record.

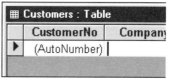

4 You can't write anything in the first field, as it contains the customer's serial number. Press ⟵ to go to the next field.

5 Enter the name of the first company and then press ⟵.

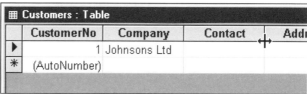

6 The field for the contact name is a bit too small. Move the cursor to the right-hand column margin, ...

57

	CustomerNo	Company	Contact		Add
▶	1	Johnsons Ltd			
✳	(AutoNumber)				

7 ... hold the mouse key down and drag it to the right to make the column wider.

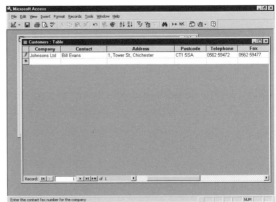

8 Now enter the first complete record. Use ⏎ to move the cursor to the next field each time.

▦ Customers : Table

	CustomerNo	Company	Contɑ
	1	Johnsons Ltd	Bill Evans
▶	(AutoNumber)		

9 When you have made your last input in the last field of this record, press ⏎. The cursor will jump to the first field of the second record and you can start entering the next customer's details.

And here are some more customers for you to enter in your customer table:

Customer No	Company	Contact	Address	Town	Postcode	Telephone	Fax
1	Johnsons Ltd	Bill Evans	1, Tower St	Norwich	NH1 5SA	0792 59472	0792 59477
2	ACTRO Computers	Andrew Gardner	Actro House, High Road	Norwich	NH5 1QT	0792 458450	0792 458450
3	Eves & Pearson	Wendy Eves	Suite 4, The Globe, Midway	York	YK6 0HH	0668 842212	0668 842241
4	SmartSync plc	Carol McCormack	Unit 12, Sutton Park	Swansea	SA16 4AP	0912 774077	0912 774077
5	Thomson (UK) Ltd	Marcus Lloyd	18, Drovers Way	London	NW1	081 468 1281	081 468 7339
6	Bits 'n PCs	Andrea Wright	49, Mead Gardens	York	YK4 4FJ	0668 548989	0668 548989
7	ID Peripherals	Ian Davies	1b, Sand Trading Estate	Swansea	SA11 5LK	0912 715715	0912 715716

To change the contents of a field, select it and press function key F2 . Now you can move the cursor to the text you want to change.

Once you have finished entering all the records, just close the table. To do this, click on the cross in the top right-hand corner of the window or select FILE/CLOSE.

Were you expecting Access to ask you if you wanted to save the changes, perhaps? As soon as you add records to a table, they are saved to the current database. As soon as the cursor disappears from the line, Access adds the new customer to the database. Of course, this makes for more safety when entering data – and above all, it means that a number of users can be working on the same database at once.

Look at the record flag on the far left of the line you are working on: if it looks like a pencil, it means the record is being edited. If it is a black triangle, the line has been saved complete to the database.

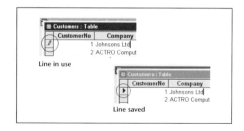

59

Finding your way around a table

As time goes by, the number of records in the table will grow, and very soon there will be more records than the screen can show. To go to a particular record, or simply scroll through the records, the best thing is to use the record navigator. That is, the cursor key boxes in the lower left-hand corner of the table.

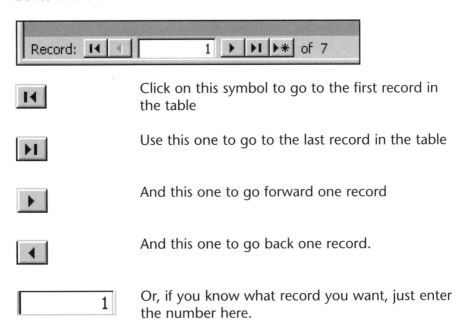

Record: ◄◄ ◄ [1] ► ►I ►* of 7

◄◄	Click on this symbol to go to the first record in the table
►I	Use this one to go to the last record in the table
►	And this one to go forward one record
◄	And this one to go back one record.
[1]	Or, if you know what record you want, just enter the number here.

Changing the table structure

Although you have already entered data in your customers' table, you can change the structure of the table, i.e. the number, names and order of field names, at any time. Just add new fields to the table and then enter the data in datasheet view. The strict separation between the two views, design view and datasheet, means you can make these changes at any time. (Actually, 'at any time' is a bit of an exaggeration – once you've linked the table to other tables, you shouldn't change the structure.)

Now try making some changes to your customers' table:

▪ First, reduce the sizes of the text fields 'Company' and 'Town' to 30 characters. That's quite enough.

▪ Now you need two new fields, *Email* and *Internet*. Use the *Email* field to enter the customer's email address, and *Internet* for their home page if they have one. Make this field a *Hyperlink* type field.

▪ Now you want another field to show the customer's marital status, but you want to have a list of possible options (single, married, etc.)

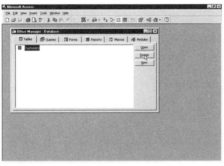

1 Highlight your table in the database window and open it in design view.

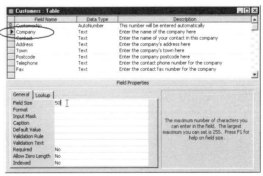

2 Move the cursor and flag the *Company* field. Move the flag to the field characteristics field.

61

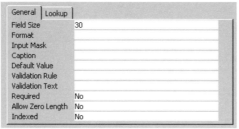

General	Lookup	
Field Size	30	
Format		
Input Mask		
Caption		
Default Value		
Validation Rule		
Validation Text		
Required	No	
Allow Zero Length	No	
Indexed	No	

3 ... and change the field size. Enter '30' and press ⏎. Then do the same for the field sizes for the *Town* field.

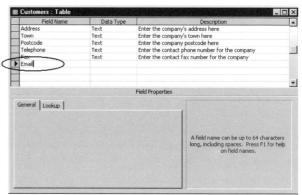

4 Move the cursor to the first field of the next vacant line and enter a new field name.

5 The *Text* field data type is confirmed, and you can enter the description again in the last field on the line.

6 The next field is called *Internet* and the field type is *Hyperlink*. Give this field a good description too.

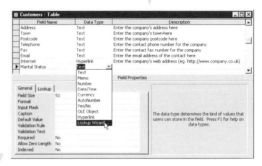

7 On the next line, enter *Marital status*. For this field, use the Lookup Wizard.

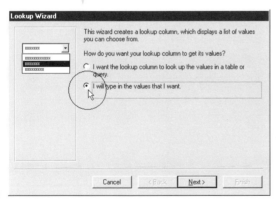

8 When the wizard starts, select the second option, as you do not have a table containing the contents of the list.

63

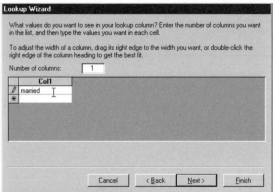

9 The list is single-column as you wanted. Now enter the first text anyone using this table will be able to select in this field.

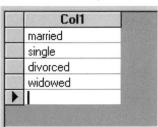

10 Using the [⇥] key, move down a line and enter the next item on the last line. Do this until you have entered all options.

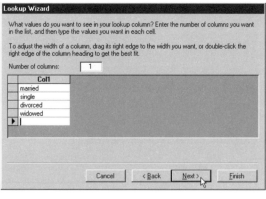

11 Once you have entered the last item on the list, click on *Next* to confirm.

12 Now you can give the field a name. This will also be used as the column heading. Click on *Finish* to close the field definition.

You can save your table design again by clicking on the floppy disk icon. You can use the top left-hand icon to switch to recording data in datasheet view and add data for individual customers. If you move the cursor to the *Marital status* field, you'll see a little arrow icon appear to the right of it. Clicking on this shows the pull-down menu you set up using the Lookup Wizard.

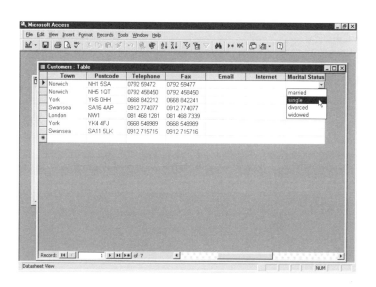

65

This new field data type, *Hyperlink*, is also interesting. If you put an entry into the *Internet* field, the system converts it to a hyperlink automatically. A hyperlink is a link to an Internet page or another document in one of the Office programs. Move the cursor to this hyperlink (hyperlinks are always underlined in blue), and you'll see it change to a hand; just click once, and this will take you to that Internet page or Office document (Word file, Excel table etc.). To link to an Internet page, of course, you will need to have a modem or ISDN adapter installed and an Internet access account set up.

Here are a list of field data types that you can use in designing tables:

Data type	Description	Maximum size
Text	For all kinds of text and numbers as symbols, not for use in calculations	255 bytes
Memo	Longer texts, descriptions, remarks on the record	65,535 bytes
Number	Numbers and figures	4 bytes (single) 8 bytes (double)
Date/Time	Date and time. The date runs from 100 to 9999	8 bytes
Currency	For currency amounts, accurate to four decimal places	8 bytes
AutoNumber	Automatically generates serial numbers	4 bytes

Data type	Description	Maximum size
Yes/No	Can only be Yes or No	1 bit
OLE Object	Images and objects from other programs	1 Gigabyte
Hyperlink	Text to be used as hyperlink address	2,048 characters a line
Lookup Wizard	Produces a pull-down list with the values you specify or from other tables	Field size in other table

Changing the table layout

The table layout is how the table appears, but of course that doesn't always have to be the same. Just as when you recorded your first data, you can make columns wider or narrower, add and remove columns and even change column headings if you want to. Let's try making a few changes to the customer table:

Move the cursor to the line between the first and second columns in the table.

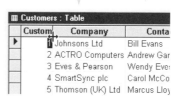

Now press the left-hand mouse key, hold it down and drag and drop the column to the left. The column will get narrower when you release the mouse key.

67

3 Now move the cursor to the *Contact* column.

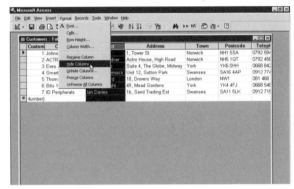

4 From the FORMAT menu, select HIDE COLUMNS.

5 You can use the menu command UNHIDE COLUMNS to show the column again.

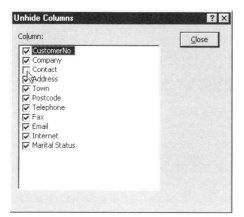

Highlight the column you want to put back in and click on OK to confirm.

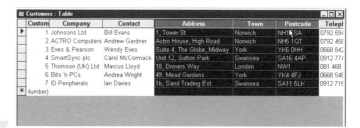

To remove a number of columns, highlight each column heading by moving the mouse across the field names.

Double-click to give a column the ideal width (i.e. so the column is just wide enough to hold the longest entry)

69

If, once you've changed the layout, you close the table by clicking on the *Close* icon in the top right-hand corner or by using the CLOSE command from the FILE menu, a message will appear:

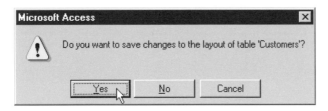

You want to save the changes. Don't forget you are not changing any data in the database, but the design of an object.

Sorting data

Of course, tables are not the only way of displaying data, but have the advantage that they can be edited using a lot of different software tools to give them the form you want. For instance, you could sort your customer data by one of the fields, let's say by company name or place, and then print the sorted table out on a printer. With Access, you can sort data in ascending or descending order, and even sort by more than one column.

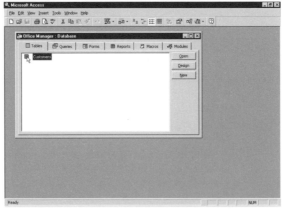

 Call up your table in the database window by double clicking on the table name.

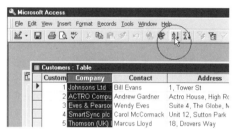

To sort the table alphabetically by company names, put the cursor in column 2 ...

... and click on the symbol in the symbol bar to sort by rising order.

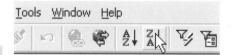

The second symbol sorts the list in descending order. Once again, the criterion is the field in which the cursor is positioned.

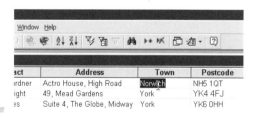

Let's try another field: sort the table by place names (only one field to highlight).

71

Filtering tables

Say you want to make the table up so it only shows customers from a given area, or you want to display a given group of records only. This is where filters come in. You can set up a filter for a table and switch it on and off any time you want. You can even save filters and then retrieve them for the table as you need them.

The filter types available are as follows:

  Selection-based filters: just highlight the record you want to use as the default for all the others.

  Form-based filters: these are filter criteria you enter in a separate window for the whole table.

  Special filters: a query window which you can use to set up filter criteria with logic characters such as =, > and <.

With our first filter, we're going to set up the table so it only shows customers from Swansea. So, first we are going to use a selection-based filter:

Address	Town	Postcode	Tel
Actro House, High Road	Norwich	NH5 1QT	0792
49, Mead Gardens	York	YK4 4FJ	0668
Suite 4, The Globe, Midway	York	YK6 0HH	0668
1b, Sand Trading Est	Swansea	SA11 5LK	0912
1, Tower St	Norwich	NH1 5SA	0792
Unit 12, Sutton Park	Swansea	SA16 4AP	0912
18, Drovers Way	London	NW1	081 4

1 Move the cursor to the Town field, to the record for one of your customers from Swansea.

2 Select the menu command
RECORDS/FILTER/FILTER BY SELECTION.

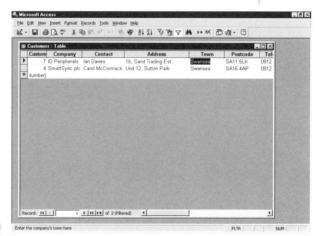

3 The table has now been filtered: it
only shows customers from Swansea.

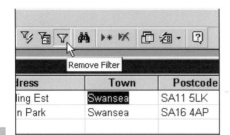

4 On the toolbar, you will now see an icon of a funnel. The tooltip at the cursor position tells you what the button does.

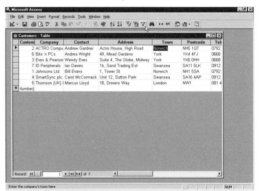

5 Click on the button, and the selection-based filter is removed. The table is now displayed in full.

You can also use **selection-based filters** via the filter icon from the toolbar – but don't forget to highlight the table first!

The second kind of filter is not much more complicated – you just have to enter the criterion in a table field. Use form-based filters to sort customers by a given area, for example:

Select the menu option RECORDS/FILTER BY FORM.

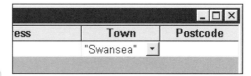

The table is now down to one line, and the system suggests the filter criterion you used last time. Enter the town "Swansea".

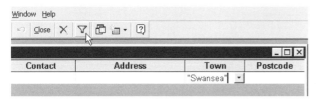

Click on the filter button to filter by this criterion.

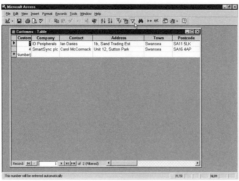

4 The table is now filtered. To remove the filter, click on the filter button again.

Quick progress check

Look at the list of questions below, and put a cross in the True or False column depending on what you think the right answer is. (Of course, you can always go back and look in the text if you're not sure.)

Question	True	False
1 A database can only have one table.		
2 The file extension MDB indicates an Access database.		
3 A fieldname can be up to 20 characters in length.		
4 There are an infinite number of field data types.		
5 The primary key means the field which occurs in all the tables.		

Question	True	False

6 When entering data in a table, pressing ⌐ always takes you to the next record.

7 You use F2 to open a highlighted field (the field with the cursor flashing in it).

8 If you see a pencil to the left of a record, it means the record has already been saved.

9 To move around in the database, use the navigator arrow keys in the lower left-hand corner of the table window.

10 You cannot use numbers in text-type fields.

11 You can only sort tables in ascending order.

12 A selection-based filter sorts a table by the criterion you displayed before you called it up.

13 A filter stays with a table even after that table is closed.

14 Telephone numbers are numbers, and should be put in numerical fields.

15 A *Hyperlink* field makes entries into Internet links.

You'll find the answers in the appendix.

3

Address management

What's in this chapter?

In this chapter, you'll meet the database wizard, which will help you set up your database all the way through, step by step. Wizards can help enormously when designing a database. Using an address book as an example, you'll learn how the wizard can help you and how to use the objects in the database (tables, forms and reports) that you set up. At the same time, you'll learn how to edit and design forms and reports.

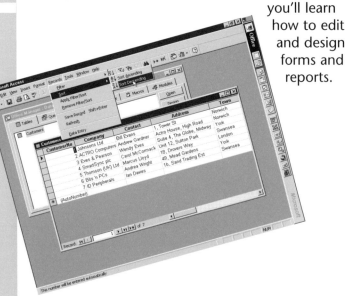

You already know:

You are going to learn:

Using the wizard to set up a new database

While you were working through chapter 2 and setting up a new database and your first table, you may have noticed that using the software is not the hardest part. The hardest part is carefully planning in advance: What fields should a table contain?, What kinds of data will it need?, How much data is involved? and so on.

This is where the database wizard can take a whole load of work off your hands. You can use it to design complete tables: it suggests what fields to use, all you have to do is choose. Let's see if it can offer us an address book.

> Whether you make up a database using the wizard or do it yourself, the end result is the same: a file with the **extension MDB** (Microsoft Database), containing one or more tables. The only difference is, the wizard can help you design tables and set up forms and reports.

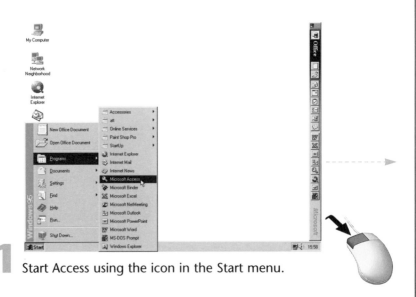

Start Access using the icon in the Start menu.

The start dialog offers the databases already set up. Select the Database Wizard ...

... and click on OK to confirm.

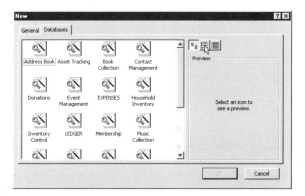

The screen shows the different wizards available: the first wizard is already highlighted. You can view the selection differently. Click on the middle button.

81

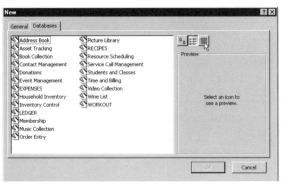

5 This is the list display, or you can also display by wizards ...

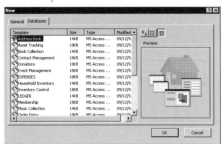

6 ... with additional details, such as file size. Once again, highlight the first wizard from the list ...

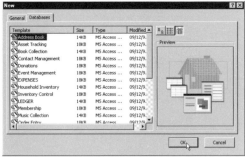

7 ... and open your new database.

8 The system now asks you what you want to call your new database. Enter 'Address Manager'.

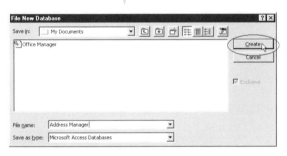

9 Confirm the name ...

10 ... and the wizard will get to work. The database window is already set up and the first dialog field appears.

83

Now let's see how the wizard sets up the database automatically:

1 In the first dialog, the wizard shows what tables it will set up. This wizard can only set up one table, i.e. address details.

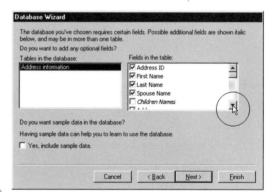

2 Here are the fields this table will contain. Scroll down the list ...

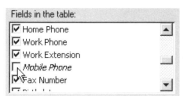

3 ... and you'll find that the suggestions not included are shown in italics. Let's say you want to include mobile phone numbers in your list.

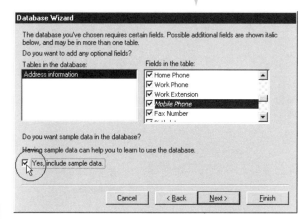

4 You should include sample data in the database so you can check the tables straight away.

5 Now go on to the next step.

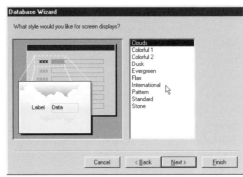

6 Now you can select the style you want, which specifies the background, colours and fonts the form will be using. Why not take a look at other suggestions, such as *International*, ...

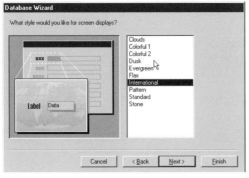

7 ... which includes graphics?

8 And Dusk gives an interesting night-time view.

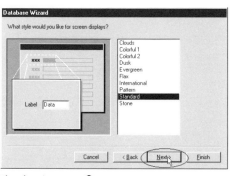

9 The basic
style is less exciting
but easier to use.
We'll use this one.

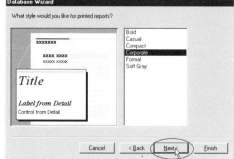

10 You can also specify a style
for reports which selects the fonts for
the heading and subheadings and
puts in lines in the right places. Let's
use this suggestion.

11 Now you can enter the name you want to use in
the table, form and report. The image in the report could be
your company's logo (but you need to have it on file).

87

What would you like the title of the database to be?

Addresses

12
Enter the name you want ...

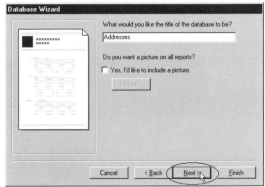

13
... and confirm this dialog field.

14
Then complete the wizard's work by clicking on *Finish*.

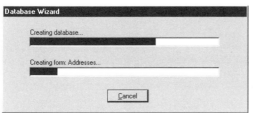

15 Now it'll take a little while for the wizard to set up all the objects in the database …

16 … but, finally, you'll see the new database with a summary form. All you have to do is select the object you want.

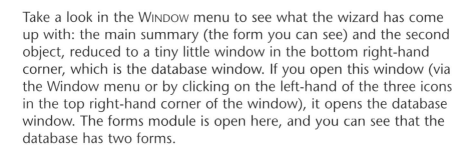

Take a look in the WINDOW menu to see what the wizard has come up with: the main summary (the form you can see) and the second object, reduced to a tiny little window in the bottom right-hand corner, which is the database window. If you open this window (via the Window menu or by clicking on the left-hand of the three icons in the top right-hand corner of the window), it opens the database window. The forms module is open here, and you can see that the database has two forms.

89

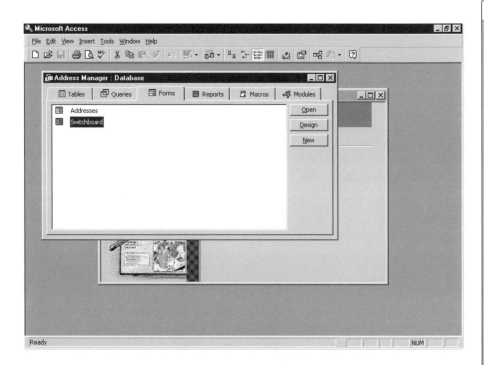

There are also two entries in the tables module. The first table is the address book itself; the second is used for the summary form, but you don't need to bother about that here.

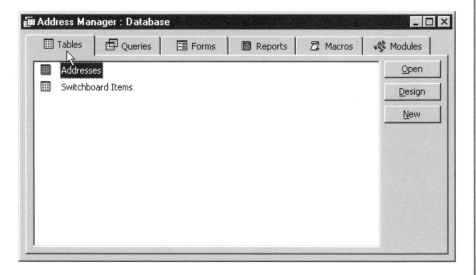

There's something in the reports module too. Switch to this tab in the database window, and you'll find the wizard has automatically generated some reports, including an address list, a list of birthdays and even an automatic greetings card for each address from the address book.

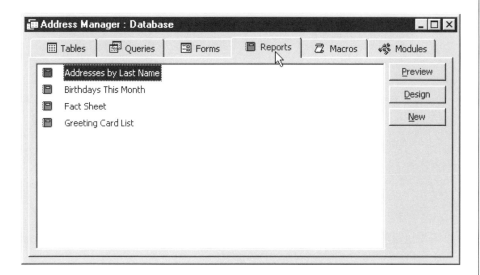

Changing the table structure

Of course, you can change the structure of the address table any way you like, but you should do this before you start putting any data in it. Look at the fields and their characteristics and see if they're what you want. Delete anything you don't need, and add any new fields you may require.

What about a validity rule for a field? This is to ensure that only the data you want gets entered in this field.

1 The database window is active. Double-click to open the table.

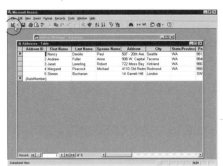

2 The table shows the sample data. Click on the button in the top left-hand corner to switch to the structure.

Field Name	Data Type
🔑 AddressID	AutoNumber
FirstName	Text
LastName	Text
→ SpouseName	Text
Address	Text
City	Text
StateOrProvince	Text
PostalCode	Text
Country	Text
EmailAddress	Text
HomePhone	Text

⊞ Addresses : Table

3 If you want to delete a line (e.g. the Spouse Name), click the row button at left of the line.

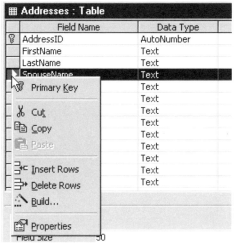

4 Click the right-hand mouse button to highlight the line and open the menu at the same time

5 Use this option to delete the line.

6 As a precautionary measure, the system asks you to confirm that you want to delete this field.

93

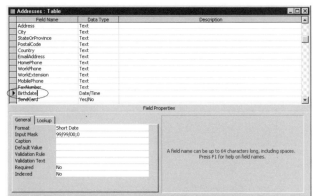

7 The field has now been deleted, along with any data in it. Now highlight the Birthdate field.

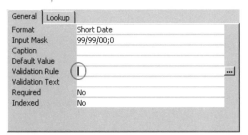

8 Add a validity check. The date in this field should not be later than today's date. Click on the blank field.

9 Open the form editor ...

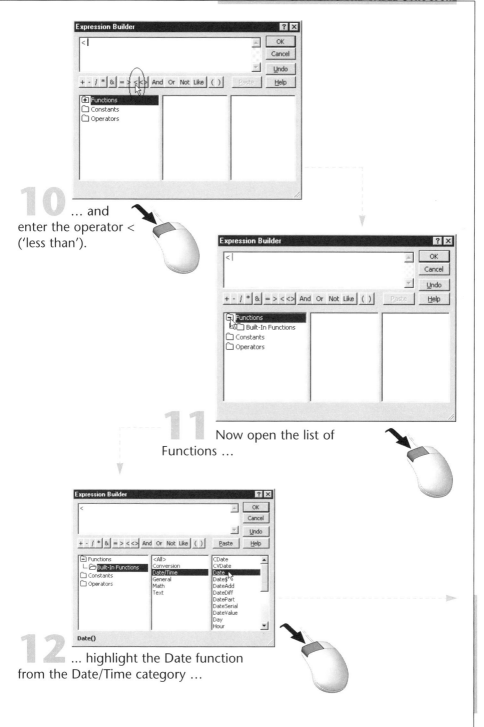

10 ... and enter the operator < ('less than').

11 Now open the list of Functions ...

12 ... highlight the Date function from the Date/Time category ...

95

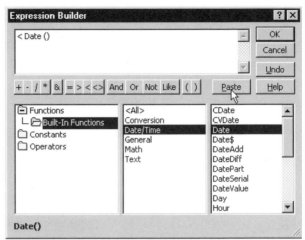

13 ... and add the function to the form. Then click on OK to close.

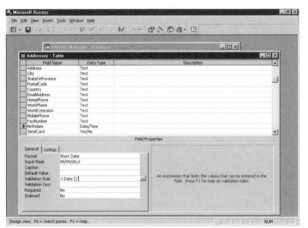

14 We now have a validity rule: the date entered must not be later than today's date. You have now set up the form, you can switch to datasheet mode and record data.

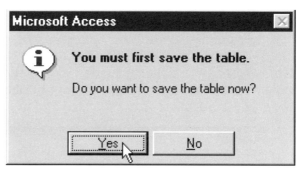

15 But hold on, you've got to save the table first.

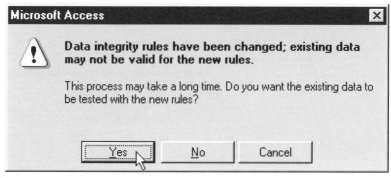

16 OK, you can confirm this too, you haven't broken any rules.

You can also add a validity message to the field characteristics. This message will then appear if an entry violates the validity rule.

Using forms

A form is a mask in which you enter data to go into a table. Each form is based on a table or query: it shows the individual records it contains and allows you to scroll through them, amend the data and add new records.

1 The address database has a form that allows you to call up the edit form. Click on the first option.

2 There are too many form fields to fit in the window all at once. We need to make the window longer.

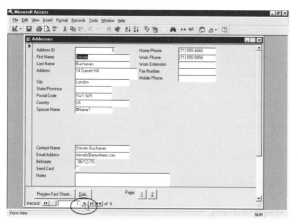

3 Now you can scroll through the records, by clicking on the record navigator keys.

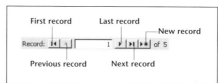

First record   Last record
                                New record
Record: |◄| ◄| 1 ►|►||►*| of 5
Previous record   Next record

4 You can scroll up or down one record at a time or go to the start or the end of the table. Use the star icon to delete the mask for the next new record.

Address ID	5
First Name	Steven
Last Name	Buchanan
Address	14 Garrett Hill
City	London
State/Province	
Postal Code	SW1 8JR
Country	UK
Spouse Name	#Name?

5 To go down to the next field in the form, use ↓ or ↵.

6 Enter the next record.

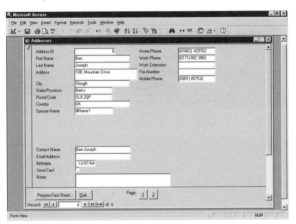

7 Enter the address data in the fields and press ⏎ to close each field.

8 If you go to the next or previous record, this record is saved automatically.

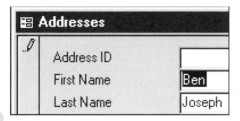

9 Look at the record display. The pencil shows that the record has not been saved yet.

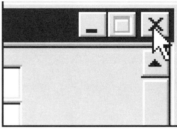

10 Once you have entered all the records, close the form.

You can also edit forms in datasheet mode. Use the familiar icon in the top left-hand corner of the screen to switch display modes. The wizard has also included a datasheet mode box in the form.

What you see in datasheet mode looks much the same as a table, but in fact it's a form. You can enter data here just as you would in a table; and, once again, you can see the record navigator in the lower left-hand corner of the window. Use the button in the top left-hand corner to switch back to the form, or click on the cross in the upper right-hand corner of the window to close the datasheet.

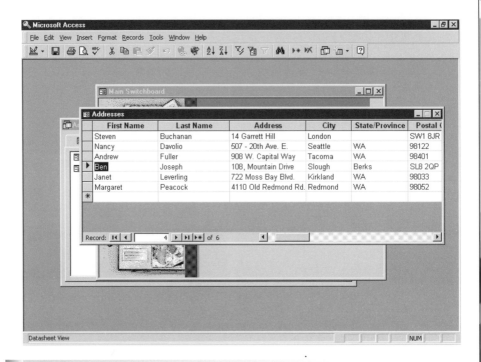

Changing the form design

Controls are what we call the fields in a form that show the individual columns in a table record by record.

Now it's time to change the form. We are going to get rid of the controls we don't want and change the wording and format of the form as well.

1 Close the form window so the summary list appears. Double-click on the title of the database window ...

2 ... and the window is now active. Now switch to the Forms tab.

3 Highlight the Addresses form ...

103

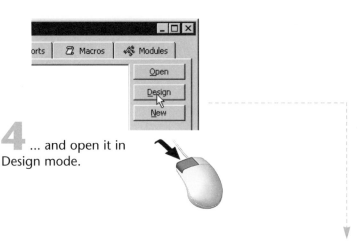

4 ... and open it in Design mode.

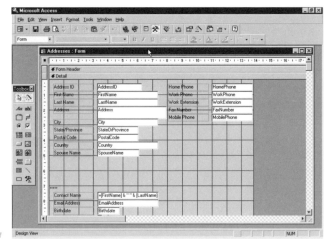

5 The form is now open, and you can see the names and text fields in the input field.

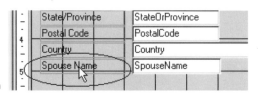

6 Select this field name which is not in the table ...

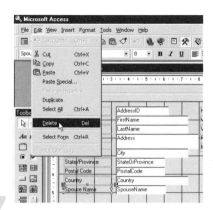

7 ... and delete it from the form design.

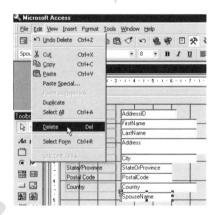

8 Now delete the input field as well.

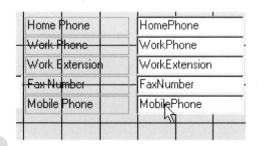

9 To move a field around, drag and drop it (i.e. click the mouse on it and hold the key down)...

105

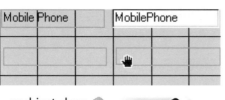

10 ... and just drag the two elements down.

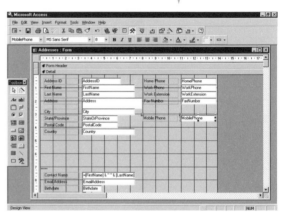

11 Now you can save the new form design...

12 ... and switch to Form View to continue editing the data.

Editing and printing forms

As well as the form for entering and editing data, the database wizard has set up a number of reports. Reports are output masks: you don't enter any data in a report field until you want to print it. Let's take a look at the reports in the address database.

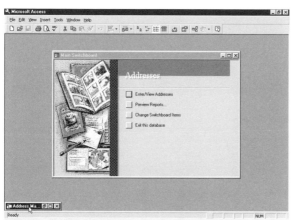

1 Close the form, reactivate the database window ...

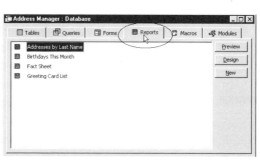

2 ... and switch to the Reports tab.

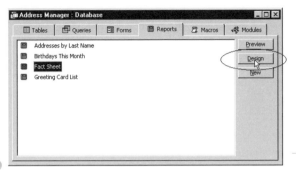

3 Highlight the Fact Sheet
and open the Design view.

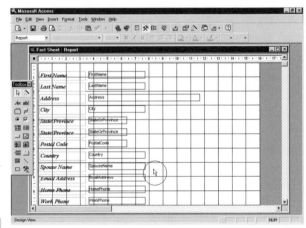

4 Once again, you can delete any fields you
don't need. Put the cursor next to the field ...

5 ... and draw a frame
around both elements.

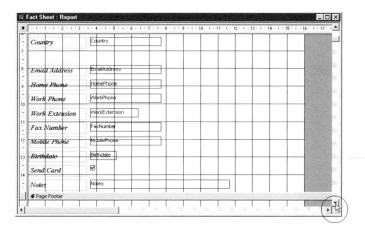

6 Now you can delete both elements by pressing the `Delete` key. Use the page scroll bar to scroll the report upwards.

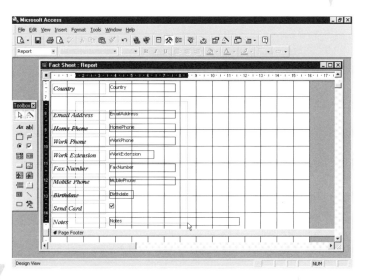

7 Now select the second group of elements ...

109

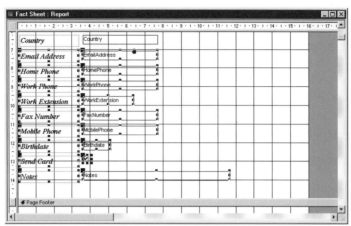

8 ... and move these elements up.

9 Now look at the report in page view.

10 This is how the report will look when printed. The cursor changes into a magnifying glass, and you just click ...

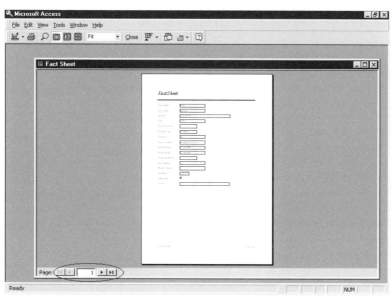

11 ... to zoom the display to full page size. You can scroll through the report by using the cursor keys in the bottom left-hand corner of the report and print it out using the printer icon.

The report automatically contains all the data from the table. If you add new addresses, just print the report again. Now you can take a look at the other reports in the reports module, open them in design mode and move the elements around.

Quick progress check

Got all that? This exercise is designed to help you recapitulate the main terms and procedures. Go on, it's worth it! Just tick what you think is the right answer in each case.

Question	Answer
1. You start the database wizard ...	a) by opening a database b) by starting Access c) after your evening meal
2. The wizard offers a number of different styles for the screen. What this means is	a) the length of the records b) establishing the database size c) formatting the screen forms, with fonts and background
3. If a wizard sets up a database, this contains	a) a database window with tables, forms and reports b) no database window, just forms c) data only
4. The validity rule for a table field indicates	a) how quickly the field is to be displayed b) what a user can put in the field c) what font is used for the field
5. A form is a mask for entering ...	a) all the tables in a database b) an individual table (or query) in a database c) refunds of travel costs

Question	Answer
6. 'Controls' are ...	a) the monthly data for the tax office
	b) the fields in the table design
	c) the fields in the form design
7. A report always contains ...	a) all the data from the underlying table or query
	b) a list of all files on the hard disk
	c) all the control elements in a form
8. The *Date()* formula which can be used in the validity rule ...	a) changes the date back one day
	b) contains today's date
	c) blocks today's date so it can't be used at all
9. The summary list window the wizard produces is...	a) an error in the program
	b) a form
	c) a report
10. There are three boxes in the top right-hand corner of the database window. The middle one...	a) enlarges the database window so it covers the entire workbench
	b) closes the database window and, with it, the database
	c) switches to the Solitaire game

You'll find the answers in the appendix.

What's in this chapter?

In this workshop, you'll be using another wizard to produce a relational database, changing the form structure to suit your needs again. In the form design, you'll learn about other ways of editing control elements. You'll also set up and design a form of your own, and see how to produce a report.

You already know:

You are going to learn:

115

Setting up your music collection database

You can simply merge objects from a number of different databases later on, as MDBs can contain a whole range of different objects.

Start the wizard again for your new database and follow the instructions all the way through. This will produce another MDB file with database objects like tables, forms and reports.

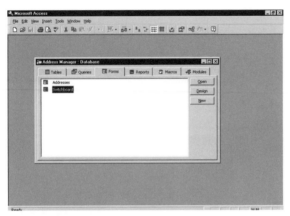

1 Once you have opened the database, just activate the FILE menu.

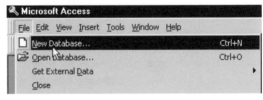

2 Open a new database.

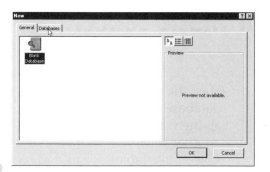

3 The open database is closed and the New window appears.

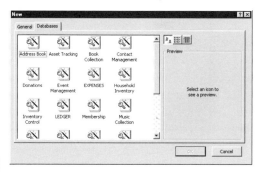

4 Now switch to the wizards display.

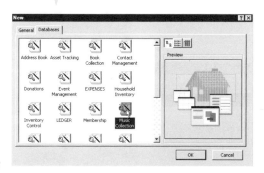

5 And double-click to start the wizard.

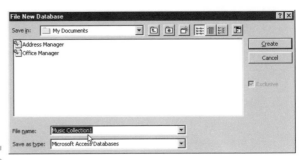

6 The system suggests a default name for the new database ...

7 ... but you give it whatever name you like. Access adds the .mdb extension itself.

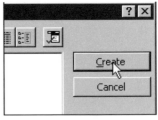

8 Now you can set up the new database.

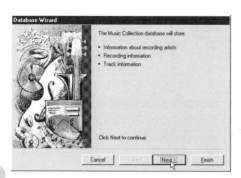

9 The database is up and running, and the wizard starts with the first question.

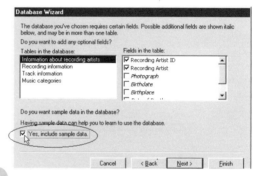

10 Look at the list of fields in the first table, highlight the one you want and include the sample data.

11 Now check the other tables and their lists of fields.

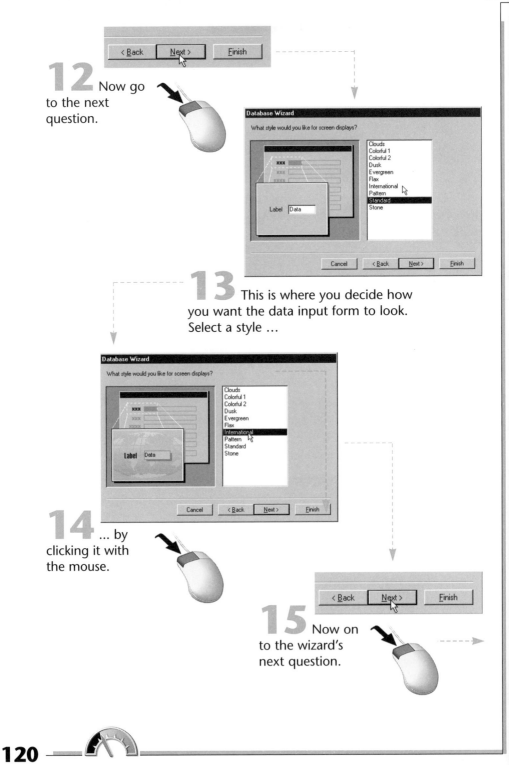

12 Now go
to the next
question.

13 This is where you decide how
you want the data input form to look.
Select a style ...

14 ... by
clicking it with
the mouse.

15 Now on
to the wizard's
next question.

16 This gives you some suggestions for designing the report. Select the first suggestion.

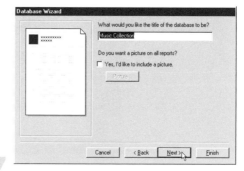

17 The next thing to do is enter the name that the tables, forms and reports are to have.

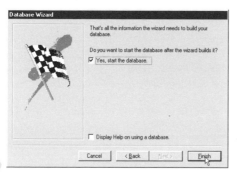

18 The wizard has all the information it needs to create your database.

121

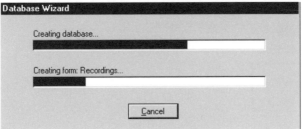

19 Now you just have to wait a little bit. Setting the objects up takes some time.

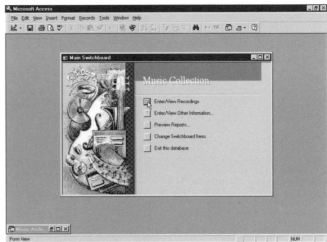

20 The database is ready. The individual objects are displayed in a summary form.

Summary forms guide people using the database to individual forms and reports. Of course, you can always open the database window and select the object you want from there.

New types of field data in the table structure

WHAT'S THIS?

Field data types tell the system what you can put in each field (e.g. 'Number', 'Date/Time', 'Currency').

As you will know from previous chapters, field structure is what everything else is based on. To ensure your database works properly, you need to use the right field data types. You'll find a list of these in the previous chapter. Now we will meet some new field data types and properties for your table.

1 In the database window, switch your new database to the tables module.

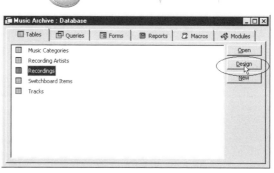

2 Open the Recordings table in Design view.

123

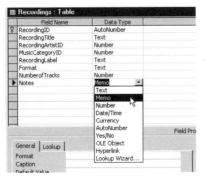

3 Now you can see a new field called *Memo* for notes.

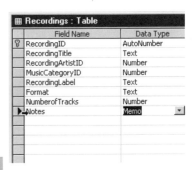

4 To add a new field in front of this field, move the cursor to the start of the previous line ...

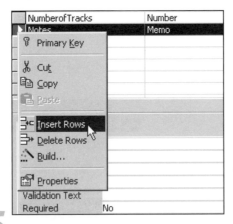

5 ... click the right-hand mouse key to select it, go to the context menu and select INSERT ROWS.

Format	Text
NumberofTracks	Number
▶ Stereo	
Notes	Memo

6 Enter the name of
the new field.

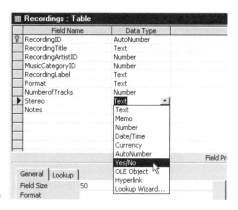

7 The field data type
here is *Yes/No*. Select it
from the list ...

8 ... and save
the new field
structure.

9 Now you can
open the table in
datasheet view ...

125

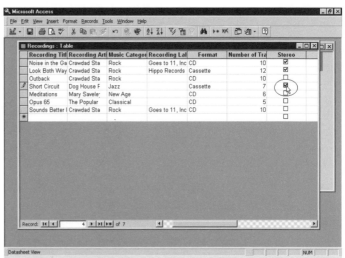

10 ...and enter the details in the individual records. Just click the mouse on the field you want.

In the field structure, you will have found a number of *numerical* type fields which refer to numbers in other tables. The Music CategoryID is a numerical field, as is the Recording ArtistID. These fields must have the *Long Integer* field size.

Now take a look at the links between tables, using the TOOLS/RELATIONSHIPS menu option.

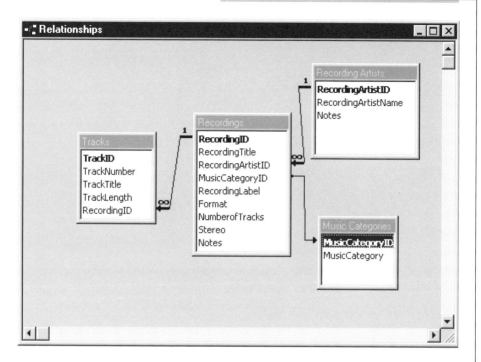

Formatting forms

Each form is divided into a number of fields. The form header shows the details that will be displayed in the header (e.g. title). The form footer is also repeated on each page; footers are mostly boxes.

Forms can also have page headers and footers, which appear on each page of the form. Lastly, the detail area shows the individual records and their fields.

Let's have a look at the record form for our music collection and add a (formatted) title to the form header.

1 To use the main form, open it in Design view from the database window.

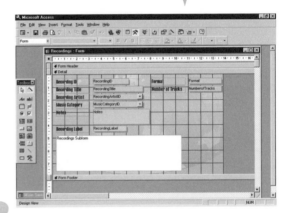

2 You can see the form header, but it's blank. Move the cursor to the bottom edge of this field ...

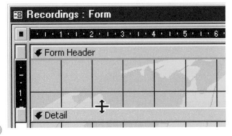

3 ... and drag it downwards to make the field larger.

5 Move the cursor (now shaped like a cross) to the top left-hand corner, ...

4 Now you can select the tool for text elements (names) from the toolbox.

6 ... click the left mouse button, hold it down and draw a rectangle the width of the form header.

7 The new element is entered. Now you can add the form's title.

129

8 Once you've finished writing the text, click in the form area and then on the box frame of the element for which you want to use a new font size.

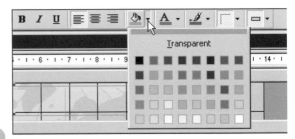

9 On the toolbar, you'll find buttons for background colour, text colour and other formatting options.

The **toolbox** is used for designing forms. If you move the cursor to a tool, a 'tooltip' tells you what that tool does.

Save the form again and switch to the datasheet view. The form now contains a title. You can also reformat elements in the form. Point to a single element, click on it, and assign it the format shown by the symbol.

If you want to reformat a number of elements, such as all lettering, use the mouse to draw a frame around all the elements you want, before you click on the format symbol.

Element properties in forms

Always use a button if there is one – it's much faster.

Each part of a form, and the form itself, has a list of properties which can be called up via the property window. You can change properties, such as font size, via this window or, alternatively, via the button on the toolbar.

This is how you list properties in the form:

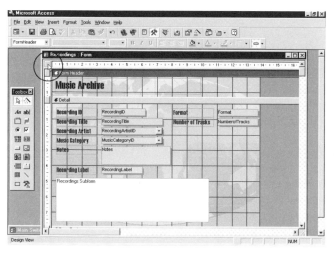

1 First, switch the form back to design view. Click on the little box in the top left-hand corner of the form window.

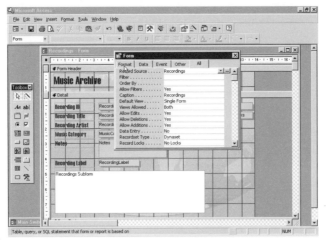

2 Double-click, and the form's property window opens.

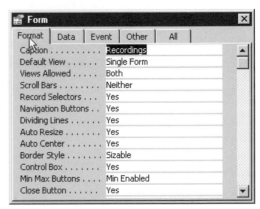

3 The *All* tab lists all properties: the other record cards are just sub-categories combining some individual groups. If you know which group a property belongs to, it's quicker to go to that group's tab than to search through the All list for it.

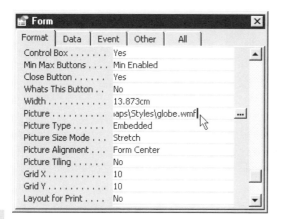

In the *Format* record card, for instance, you'll find an entry which tells you how the image in the background of the form was generated.

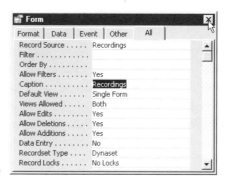

Record Source shows which tables the form is editing.

Take a look at individual elements such as this number. Select the element ...

133

7 ... and use this button to open the properties window.

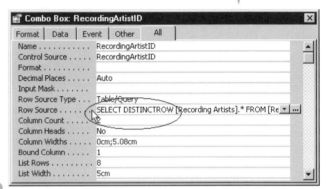

8 This formula in the record source ensures that the correct number from the other table is displayed.

9 Now save the form and close the window again.

Editing reports

As well as the tables and forms, the wizard has also set up a number of reports which you can edit or print out. Reports put the data in tables onto paper, and if you take a look at the wizard's reports, you can see there are a lot of different versions available.

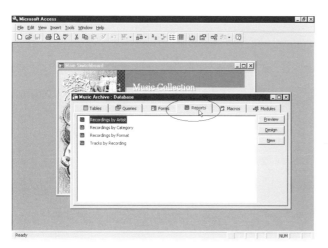

You'll find reports in the Reports module of the database window.

Open the first report by double-clicking on its icon.

135

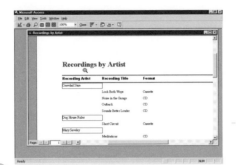

3 The report immediately appears in page view. This is how the printout will look. One click with the cursor, which now looks like a magnifying glass ...

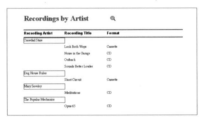

4 ... and the display is reduced to a whole page view. Now move the magnifying glass somewhere else and click to zoom the display out again.

5 To edit the report, switch to design view.

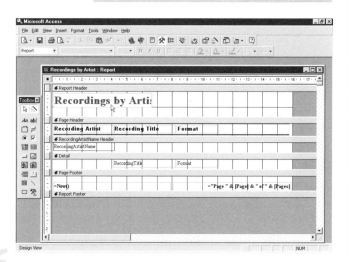

6 You will see the different report fields. Now select the header ...

7 ... and give it a larger font size.

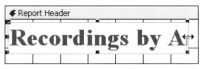

8 Now the element is too small. Double-click on the side marker ...

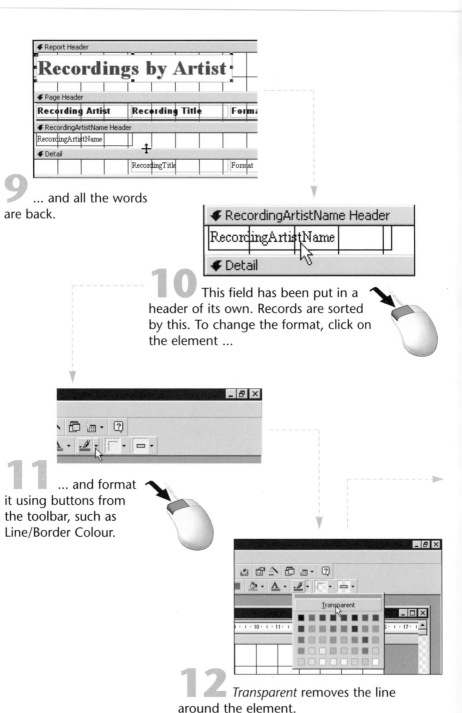

9 ... and all the words are back.

10 This field has been put in a header of its own. Records are sorted by this. To change the format, click on the element ...

11 ... and format it using buttons from the toolbar, such as Line/Border Colour.

12 *Transparent* removes the line around the element.

13 Now switch back to page view to see the results.

14 And this is how the report will look if you print it out, using the Print button.

There are some other fields of the report in the design window, but they are not difficult to make out. If you can't see a field, you can open it via the VIEW menu.

Report header	Anything in this field is printed at the top of the report.
Page header	Any fields and text elements that you enter here will be printed on each page of the report.
Header field (with field name)	This prints the field name to be used as a group. To indicate which fields are group fields, use the menu option VIEW/SORT AND GROUP.
Detail field	These are the records under the group in the header field. If no group is specified, all records will be printed.
Page footer	This gives the draft report the information to be repeated on each page (e.g. page numbers).
Report footer	This field is used to indicate what is to appear at the end of the report.

Look at the page numbers in the page footer: this is how you can set them up for each report. The wizard uses a text field and a formula (= page ...) which are entered in the properties window as control content.

Quick progress check

Now it's time for another little exercise to refresh your memory. Fill in the blanks in the text. Go back and look in the book if you can't remember something.

To set up a new database in the Access window, open the ——————— (1) menu. You can only have ——————— (2) database open at any time: any database already open will be closed when you open or set up a new one. The records have already been saved; they are saved at the time of —————— (3). The memo field can hold up to —————— (4) characters; unlike a text field, this is used for remarks and explanations. To see the links between the different tables, look under —————————— (5) in the —————————— (6) menu. Forms are divided into sections. The heading is usually in the ——————— (7), the data in the ——————— (8). To select more than one control element of the form, use the ——————— (9) to draw a box around the elements concerned. The elements ——————— (10) be enclosed in the box. To call up an element property, ——————— (11) click on the element or the *Properties* icon. Which table the form is linked to is shown by the ——————— (12) property. Reports are found in the ——————— (13) of the database window. Double-clicking on a report opens it in ——————— (14). The cursor now looks like a magnifying glass, and clicking it on the report ——————— (15) it to page view. Reports are also divided into sections: the heading is in the ——————— (16), the data in the ——————— (17). Page numbers are always found in ——————— (18).

You'll find the answers in the appendix.

5

A sports product database

What's in this chapter?

Now we're going to set up a database without the wizard's assistance. Although this will be more difficult, it will help you better understand the individual methods used and how they fit together. And, of course, the individual modules have wizards which you can always use. You'll find out the quickest way of setting up forms and reports and learn some tricks to make designing your own databases easier.

You already know:

You are going to learn:

143

A new database

Let's start by setting up a new database. Just to remind you: a database is a file that ends with the extension .MDB and contains tables, enquiries, forms, reports and possibly macros and modules. Records are saved automatically when the database is recorded, but you have to save any objects you set up to manage the database yourself.

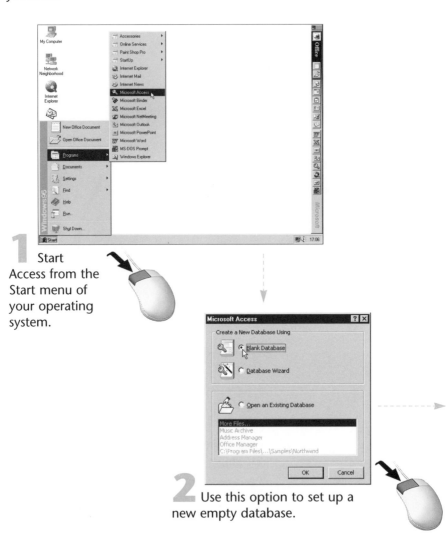

1 Start Access from the Start menu of your operating system.

2 Use this option to set up a new empty database.

3 This name can be up to 255 letters and/or numbers long. Don't add the extension; Access does that for you.

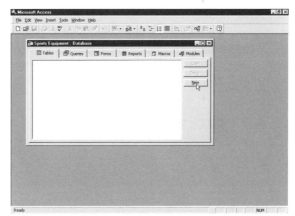

4 Your database is ready and already saved. Now you can start designing the first table.

Problems with database names?

In fact, Windows is pretty relaxed when it comes to naming files. But there are a few rules for filenames:

If you see this error message, it means you've used a slash (/), and that's not allowed.

Here's another character you're not allowed to use in a filename. Use letters, numbers, spaces and dashes only.

Table 1: Products

We will use our first table to save the products in our sports equipment database. To make sure you include all the important fields right from the start, we'll leave setting up the table structure to the wizard.

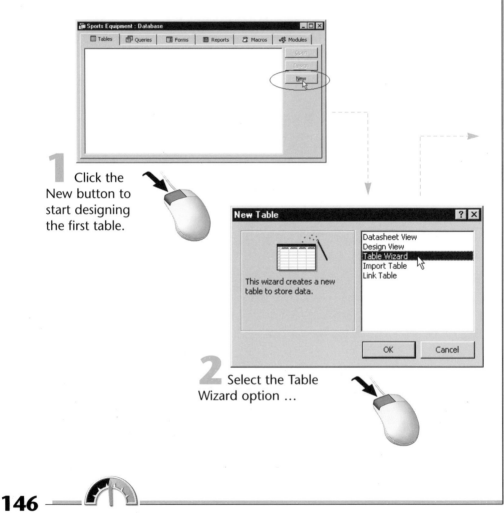

1 Click the New button to start designing the first table.

2 Select the Table Wizard option ...

3 ... and click on OK to confirm.

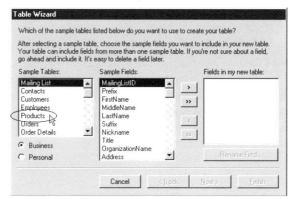

4 Now you'll see a list of sample tables, with the list of fields from the highlighted table being shown. Choose the *Products* table.

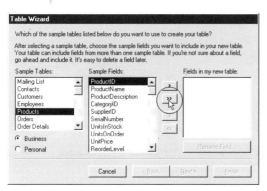

5 The field list then takes all the fields from this table. You can copy all the fields by clicking on the double arrow.

147

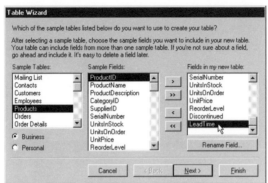

6 Now scroll through the list and look for the fields you don't need, as in this case the field *LeadTime*. Highlight the field name ...

7 ... and put the field back in the list of suggestions.

The tables wizard offers two kinds of tables. *Business* tables are those you use for, well, business, while *Personal* tables cover family or household database types.

Of course, you don't have to use the field names suggested.

If you want to give a field a different name, move it to the right-hand list, highlight it and click on *Rename Field*. Now enter the name you want to use.

If you find in another sample table a field you could use, just add it to your list. You can always add new fields in design mode at any time.

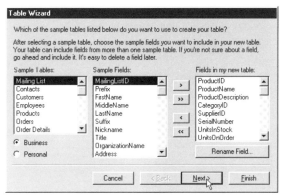

Once you have all the fields you want in the list, go to the next enquiry.

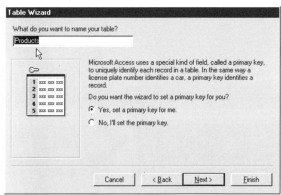

Now you have to decide what to call the table ...

What do you want to name your table?

Sports Equipment

3 Enter a name in the input field at the top.

Do you want the wizard to set a primary key for you?

● Yes, set a primary key for me.

○ No, I'll set the primary key.

4 This option makes sure that the primary key and hence another field are automatically set up at the top of the table.

< Back   Next   Finish

5 Move on ...

Table Wizard

That's all the information the wizard needs to create your table.

After the wizard creates the table, what do you want to do?

● Modify the table design.

○ Enter data directly into the table.

○ Enter data into the table using a form the wizard creates for me.

☐ Display Help on working with the table.

Cancel   < Back   Next   Finish

6 ... and take a first look at the new table in design mode.

Finish

7 Click on *Finish*, ...

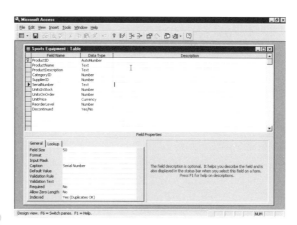

8 ... and the system offers the structure for the new table.

9 Look at the first field the wizard has set. This contains the primary key.

10 Close the structure window; the table is already saved.

11 The table module in the database window now shows the first table.

The **primary key** denotes the field that gives the record its unique indicator, and is almost always an ID field at the start of the structure. Without a primary key field, you won't be able to link a table to any others

The primary key field is always an *AutoNumber* field. This ensures that it is always updated for each new record automatically. You don't have to enter anything here, which rules out any mistakes

Take another look at the table structure in the design window and if necessary add more fields. The structure of the table should already be complete, in case you afterwards want to use the table in relation to other tables.

Table 2: Relating categories

In the structure of the product table, the product category is a numerical field, so there is no way you could enter 'ski equipment' here, for instance. Instead, you set up a separate table containing all the categories, and relate it to the first table.

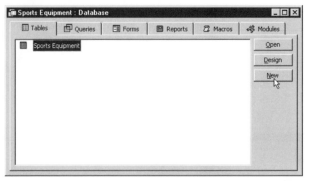

1 Once again, you set up the new table via the *New* button in the database window's Tables module.

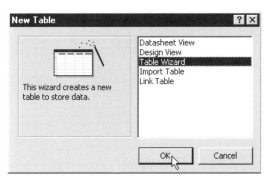

2 We'll let the Table Wizard do the work ...

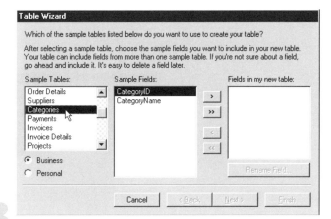

3 ... and in the *Business* category, you'll find the table you want, *Categories*.

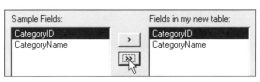

4 Add both fields to the list on the right.

153

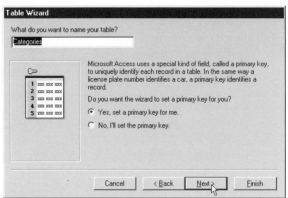

5 We'll take the name
as it stands, and the
automatic primary key.

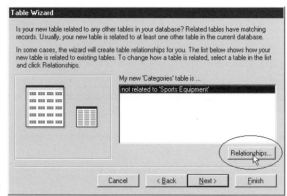

6 Now the system will
ask you another question,
because this table might
already be related to
another one. Click on
Relationships ...

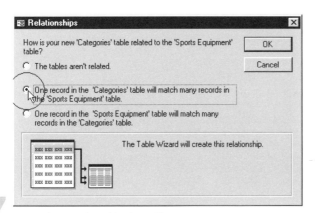

7 ... and say what kind of relationship you want. As each product category will cover a number of records, we want the second option.

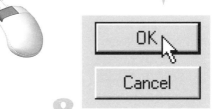

8 Confirm this dialog box ...

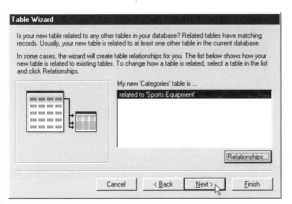

9 ... and the system adds the new relationship. Now you can go on to the next question.

155

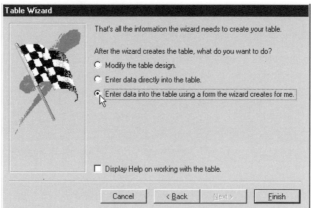

10 Our table is complete. Now you can set up a form for recording the categories.

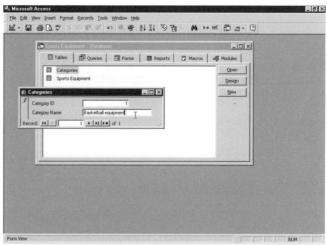

11 Let's start with the first category. Enter the name and press the ⏎ key to go to the next record (see below).

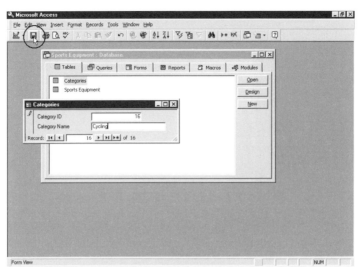

Once you've entered all the records, you can save the form.

Use the name suggested and close the form window.

Here are the categories you can enter for each form in the new table:

No.	Name
1	Basketball equipment
2	Football equipment
4	Tennis equipment
5	Rugby equipment
6	Shooting
7	Table tennis
8	Golf equipment
9	Tennis clothing
10	Football clothing
11	General clothing
12	Sports shoes
13	Training gear
14	Ice-skating
15	Skateboarding
16	Cycling

Relationships

The wizard has already linked the tables *Sports Equipment* and *Categories*. The conditions were as follows:

- A field with the name *Category no.* and field data type *Number* in the product table.

- A primary key field in the *Category* table called *CategoryID*.

To look at the relationship between the two tables, use the menu option TOOLS/RELATIONSHIPS.

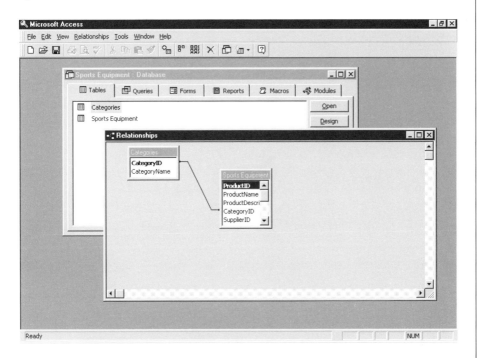

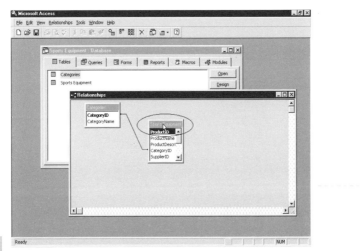

In one of the lists of fields shown, click the mouse on the header bar.

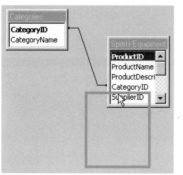

2 Pull the window in any direction you want.

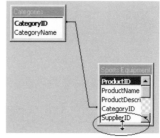

3 You can drag the border to resize the window.

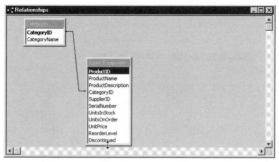

4 Dragging the border downwards lets you see its contents without scrolling.

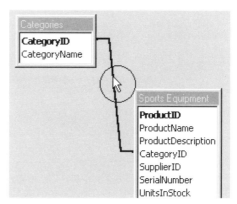

5 A click on the relationship line highlights it ...

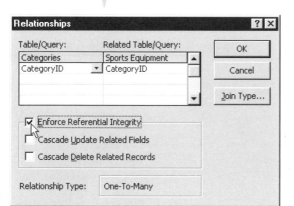

6 ... and double-clicking tells you what kind of relationship this is.

7 Now tick 'Enforce Referential Integrity' and close the window again.

161

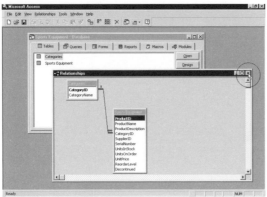

8 Now you can close the Relationships window as well.

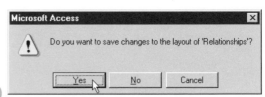

Microsoft Access ✕

⚠ Do you want to save changes to the layout of 'Relationships'?

[Yes] [No] [Cancel]

9 And you have to confirm that you want to save the new layout.

Referential Integrity means that data cannot be deleted or amended if this would put other data involved at risk. For instance, you mustn't delete a category number from the category table if it is still in the product table.

Now let's set up another table in your sporting products database. This time we'll list all the suppliers. If you use the Table Wizard, you'll find a Suppliers table in the list of suggestions. Don't forget that the SupplierID field has to have a relationship with the SupplierID number from the product table. However, there is no relationship between the category table and supplier table.

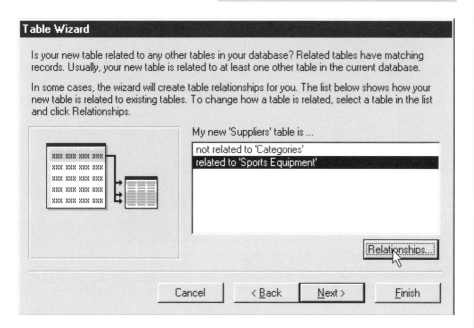

Now, let's finish by setting up a form for recording supplier data. So you can practise on it straight away, let's put some records in:

Supplier Name.	City
Niko Sports	Hong Kong
Roobock Sportsware	Los Angeles
Bedidas	London
Pumela Sport	Munich
The Trekking Company	Oslo
Kamel Sportware and Trekking	Sydney
Kucci Sport	Milan

If you made the relationship between products and suppliers correctly, the relationship window should show the new relationship.

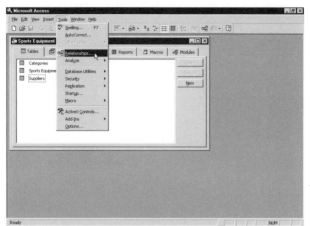

1 Let's just look through the window again using the menu option TOOLS/RELATIONSHIPS.

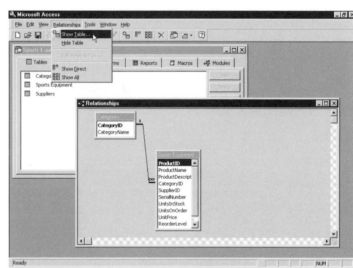

2 We can't see the new table yet; we need to add it to the window.

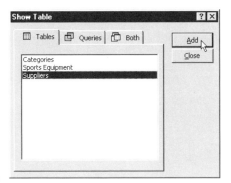

3 Highlight *Suppliers* and add the table to the window.

4 Now you can close the dialog field ...

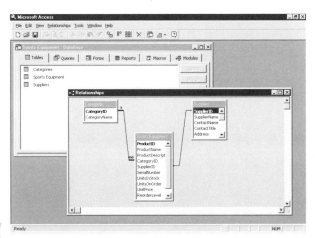

5 ... and the new relationship appears.

165

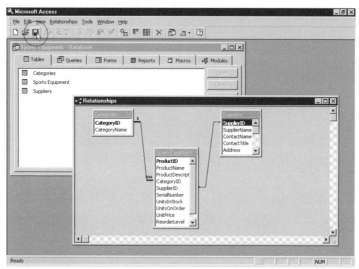

6 Save the relationships window and close it.

An AutoForm for products

You saw one way of producing a form quickly when we set up the *Categories* table. In the last question, the wizard offered you the option of switching to design or datasheet mode or using a form. If you select this option, a new unsaved form is opened for the table, and you can start entering data straight away.

You can also create these automatic forms from the main window. The quick way to set up a product data form goes like this:

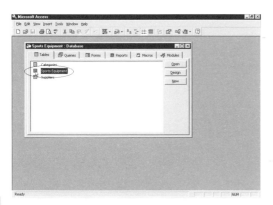

To generate a
new form for the
Sports Equipment
table, highlight it in
the database window.

Move the cursor to
this button in the top
right hand corner of the
toolbar.

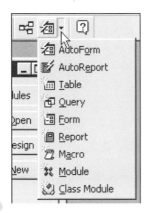

Clicking on the little
black triangle opens a list
of objects which you can
then select to set up.

167

4 We'll take the *AutoForm* option.

5 The system now sets this form up for the selected table automatically. You can save it …

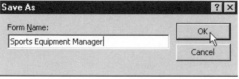

6 … and give it a suitable name.

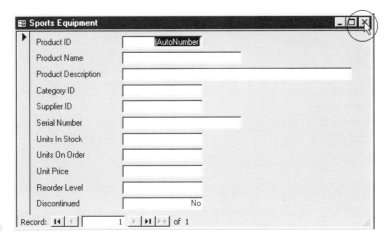

7 Now let's close the form ...

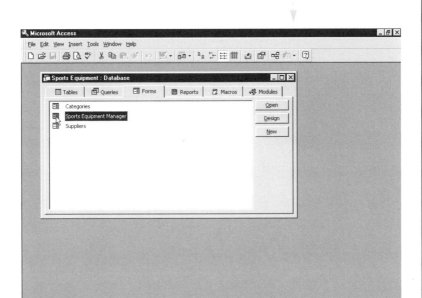

8 ... and check the Forms module in the database window. There should now be another entry here.

Combo boxes in forms

WHAT'S THIS?

The **toolbox** is the small icon bar on the left-hand side of the form design which contains tools for designing forms.

There's only one problem with *AutoForm*: it offers a list of all filenames from the table straight away, but ignores any relationships with other tables. To record the product category using the *AutoForm* set up, for instance, you'd have to know its number in the categories table and in the appropriate field. The same goes for suppliers, who are only shown as numbers in the product table.

WHAT'S THIS?

A **combo box** is an element of a form which can offer any desired content from another (related) table in list form.

Of course, this isn't what the designers intended, and the form design is prepared for this job. The solution lies in a combo box (which can be seen in the toolbox). And, as this isn't an easy thing to set up, there's another wizard to help you.

1 From the database window, open the sports equipment form in design view.

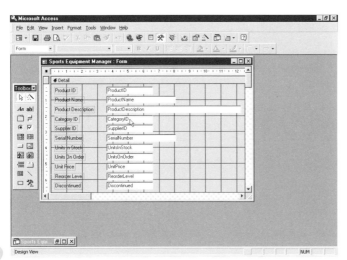

2 The individual form elements appear, with the toolbox to the left. Select the text field with the category number.

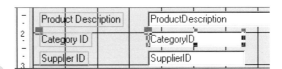

3 Now delete this field using the Delete key.

4 The element and its label are now deleted.

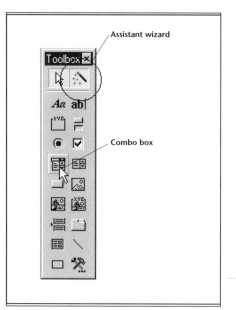

Assistant wizard

Combo box

5 Now click on the *Combo box* tool. Don't forget you need to switch the wizard on as well.

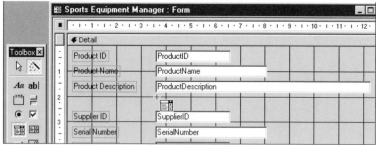

6 Using the cursor, which now has crosshair shape, click at the point where the field is to start...

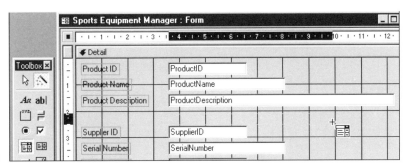

7 ...and drag a rectangle out to the size you want, keeping the mouse key pressed.

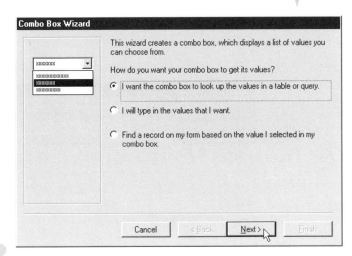

8 The field is now set up, and the wizard goes to work.

The wizard will now take you through setting up the new field step by step. The first thing it needs to know is whether the field will take its data from another table (in this case, yes, from the Categories table). So you want to answer 'yes' to the first question.

173

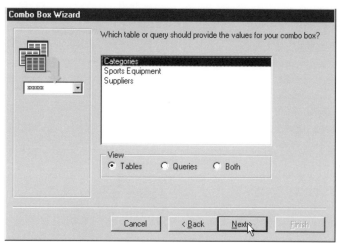

1 The table you want is the one that's already highlighted, so just click Next.

2 The next step is to say which data from the other table you want to see in your form. So highlight the category name ...

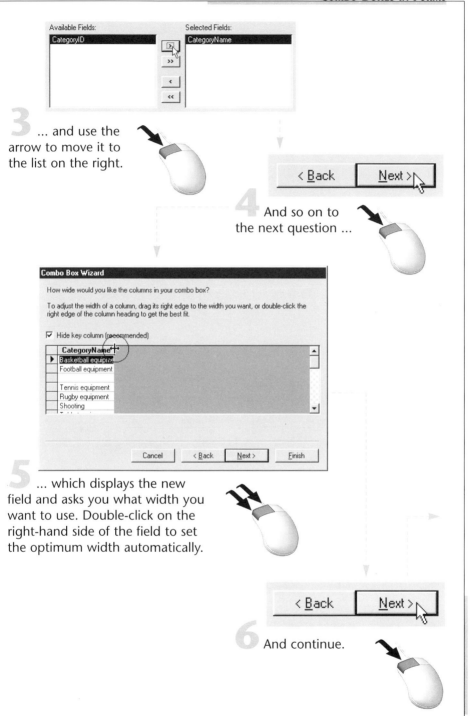

Available Fields:

CategoryID

Selected Fields:

CategoryName

3 ... and use the arrow to move it to the list on the right.

< Back   Next >

4 And so on to the next question ...

Combo Box Wizard

How wide would you like the columns in your combo box?

To adjust the width of a column, drag its right edge to the width you want, or double-click the right edge of the column heading to get the best fit.

☑ Hide key column (recommended)

CategoryName
▶ Basketball equipme
Football equipment
Tennis equipment
Rugby equipment
Shooting

Cancel   < Back   Next >   Finish

5 ... which displays the new field and asks you what width you want to use. Double-click on the right-hand side of the field to set the optimum width automatically.

< Back   Next >

6 And continue.

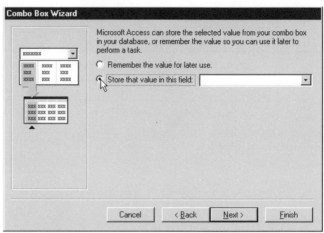

Combo Box Wizard

Microsoft Access can store the selected value from your combo box in your database, or remember the value so you can use it later to perform a task.

○ Remember the value for later use.

● Store that value in this field: [▼]

Cancel   < Back   Next >   Finish

7 Now tell the system where to save the data taken from the other table. Highlight the second option ...

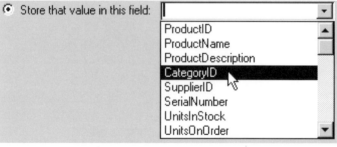

● Store that value in this field: [▼]

ProductID
ProductName
ProductDescription
CategoryID
SupplierID
SerialNumber
UnitsInStock
UnitsOnOrder

8 ... and select this field from the list.

< Back   Next >

9 Now for the wizard's final trick.

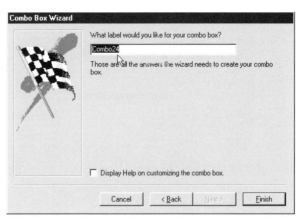

10 Here you can say what you want to call the new field.

What label would you like for your combo box?

Category

11 Enter the name ...

12 ...
and close the wizard.

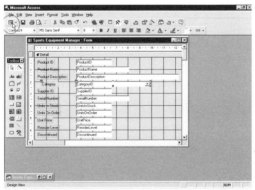

13 The new field in the form is now complete,
and you can return to entering data immediately.

177

14 The combo box now offers the categories from the Categories table, and saves the category number selected.

Got that? It isn't an easy thing to learn, but is as much a part of designing forms as relationships are in a relational database. Try it once again. The *Supplier number* field in the product form only gives you a number, whereas what you really want to see is a list of text inputs, i.e. the names of the suppliers. Go back to form design, delete the field from the form and fetch the supplier names from the other table using the wizard.

> Which field should the combo box's data be placed in? In *Supplier number*, of course.

Quick progress check

Now please take a little time to work through this exercise. Just answer the questions *True* or *False*.

Question	True	False
1 Filenames can be up to 255 characters in length.		
2 A slash is a permitted character in a filename.		
3 You must always accept all the table fields the table wizard suggests.		
4 You can rename table wizard fieldnames.		
5 You can't relate tables without primary keys.		
6 The field data type for the primary key is always Text.		
7 You can't display relationships between tables.		
8 To see the precise relationships in the relationships window, click on a line.		
9 Referential integrity ensures that data is not deleted while still in use in other forms.		
10 You can always use combo boxes to display data from other tables.		

You'll find the answers in the appendix.

What's in this chapter?

You would probably find it useful to have a database where you could record and check the birthdays of your friends, relatives and colleagues so that you need never forget a birthday again. You will also often want to filter tables against particular criteria, and the best way to do this is by using queries. This chapter will teach you how to create an employee database file and test it with various queries.

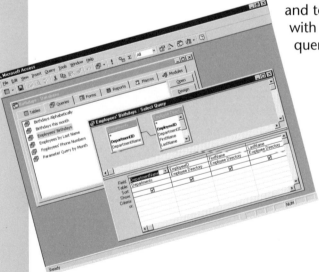

You already know:

You are going to learn:

181

Staff data table

The basis for this database could be a general database of addressees or a global database which stores the names of employees, colleagues, friends, etc. But let's create a new database and tables with relationships set up with the aid of the table wizard.

1 Start up Access from the Start menu and select the first option to create a new database.

2 Enter the name of the new MDB file ... - - - - - - - ->

3 ... and create the new database.

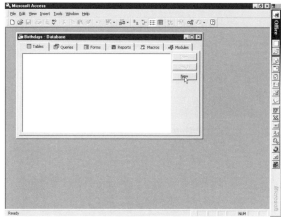

4 In the Database window begin the first table,...

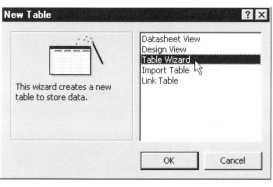

5 preferably using the table wizard to generate the structure.

183

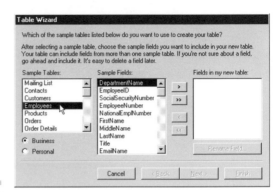

6 Select a sample table that is closest to what you want.

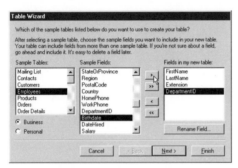

7 You don't have to include all the fields; just click on the ones that are displayed here in the list.

Sample Fields:

BillingRate
Deductions
SupervisorID
SpouseName
EmrgcyContactName
EmrgcyContactPhone
Photograph
Notes
OfficeLocation

8 If you have the facility to process photos of employees in file form, you can include a photo field as well.

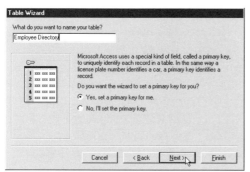

9 Now think of a suitable
name for the table ...

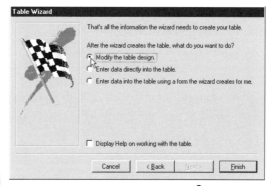

10 ... and the first table is nearly
finished. You can check the design again.

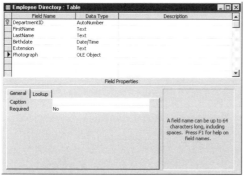

11 This is how the
table looks in design view.

185

The **OLE object** is a part of a data record that has been produced by another program called an OLE server. A picture from Corel Draw, a video, a sound file are all OLE objects which have their own data type reserved for them in the field structure.

Unfortunately, the Wizard was not able to tell what the department number was designated for and has made it the primary key field. So you must now delete the primary key by clicking on the key icon. Change the data type to *Number* with the field size *Long Integer* and save this structure.

Now insert a new row and enter the field name *EmployeeID*. The data type is set to *AutoNumber* and a click on the key icon assigns the primary key to it again. Save the changed structure and close the window again.

You must save in between because the two fields cannot be altered in one step.

▦ Employee Directory : Table	
Field Name	Data Type
🔑 EmployeeID	AutoNumber
▶ DepartmentID	Number ▾
FirstName	Text
LastName	Text
Birthdate	Date/Time
Extension	Text
Photograph	OLE Object

A linked department list

You are now going to create a second table with department names and use the relationship function to ensure that the department number from the first table is the same as the number from the second. Use the Table Wizard again; it will suggest the relationship. Create the new table as before from the database window:

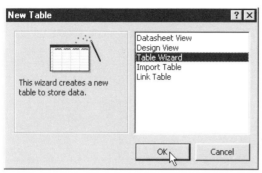

1 The table wizard will help you again.

2 Retrieve the *DepartmentID*. and *Department Name* fields from the same table as before.

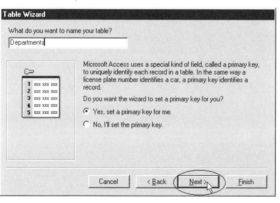

3 Give the table a name, ...

187

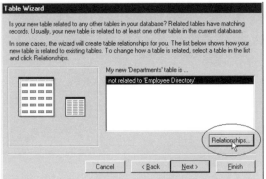

4 ... and the next step is for you to specify the relationship between the two tables.

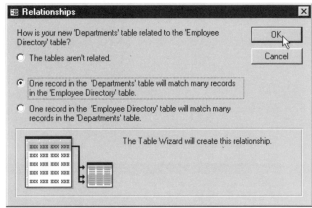

5 The second option is the one you want; several employees may work in one department.

The rest is already routine for you: save the table, close the Design and, to be on the safe side, check the relationship again via the menu command TOOLS/RELATIONSHIPS.

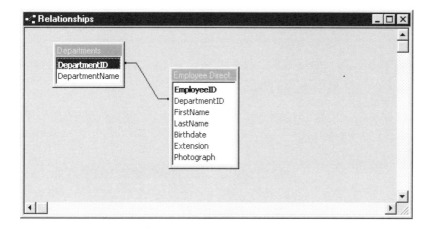

Forms for the tables

To record data you need to create forms again, but because of the relationships between the tables, these need to be changed. Begin by creating a form for the departments and then create a form to record employees. Instead of the input field for the department number, you will specify a combo box which makes the department names available.

1 For the department table, create an AutoForm from the main toolbar.

2 Save the form immediately under the suggested name.

3 For a change, let's create the second form with the help of the form wizard. Switch to the Forms module and select *New*.

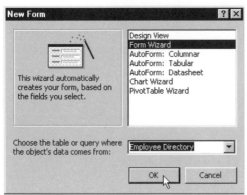

4 This will activate the wizard. Don't forget to select from the list below the table to which the form relates.

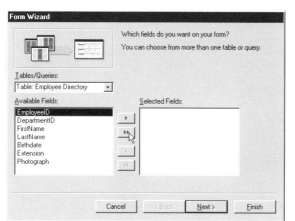

5 The next query lets you select individual fields. We need all the fields, so click on the double arrow.

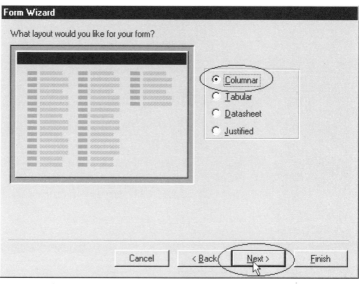

6 You need to choose the layout of the form; the single column option is the best one for our purposes.

191

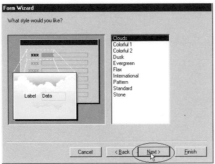

7 The next dialog field offers you some ready-made styles (font, background and colours). Select the style you want.

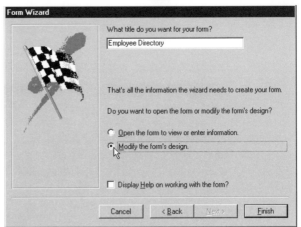

8 That's the last query from the wizard. Now you can display the form design to see if you need to make any changes.

Wizard or AutoForm? The **AutoForm** will always contain the fields arranged in a single column. If you work with the wizard, you will have greater choice of form design.

The next step is to exchange the department number field for a combo box, which provides the department names rather than numbers. Delete the *DepartmentID* field, and

192

insert a combo box. Use the Wizard to identify the relationship to the *Employee* table. The contents of the field will be stored again in the *DepartmentID.* field.

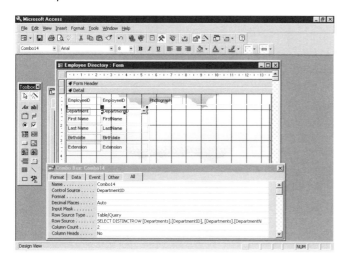

The new field appears at the bottom as the last item in the sequence and is the last one to be processed as data are recorded. Using the menu command VIEW/TAB ORDER, open a window to display the current sequence. Then drag the field to second position below the employee number.

Now you can start to enter data into your database. Begin with the department list, which you enter in the *Departments* table.

DepartmentID.	Department Name
1	Sales
2	Marketing
3	Administration
4	Customer Service
5	Production
6	Warehouse/Dispatch
7	Personnel

Record the employees on the form you have just created, which also provides department names from the combo box:

No.	Department	First Name	Last Name	Date of Birth	Extension
1	Sales	Richard	Hoover	12.1.70	211
2	Sales	David	Mayes	15.3.74	221
3	Sales	Sasha	Jameson	21.7.72	223
4	Sales	Daniel	Holland	3.11.77	224
5	Marketing	Laura	Bernard	29.3.75	332
6	Marketing	Ed	Harris	14.9.50	333
7	Marketing	William	McClelland	26.7.56	334
8	Production	Doris	Rice	3.6.58	555
9	Production	Harry	Woods	12.6.52	551
10	Production	Sharon	Delaney	16.1.62	556
11	Production	Karen	Henson	5.7.62	559

The first query

WHAT'S THIS?

Queries are stored pieces of information on the number of data records and the fields selected for incorporation in a table. Once a query has been set up and saved, it can be run at any time with current data from a table or several tables.

Let's suppose you want to generate a simple list of all the employees in all departments. Since this information is divided between two tables, you need to set up a query. Use the query wizard to help you. It will have a result for you very quickly.

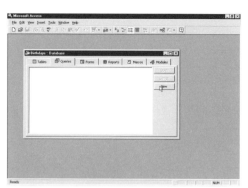

Switch to the Query module in the Database window and begin your first query.

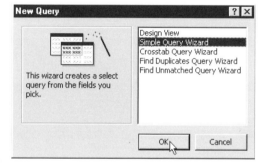

The query wizard is activated ...

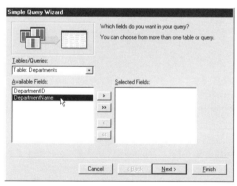

... and the next window already gives you the first table with its fields. Select the department name ...

195

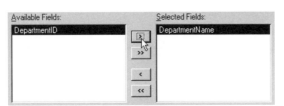

4 ... and move it over to the list of fields on the right. We don't need the department number.

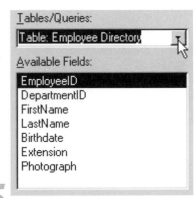

Tables/Queries:

Table: Employee Directory

Available Fields:

EmployeeID
DepartmentID
FirstName
LastName
Birthdate
Extension
Photograph

5 Switch to the second table, the *Employees.*

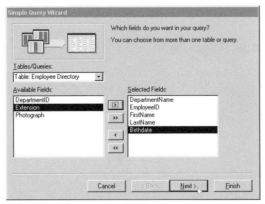

6 From this table we need only the five fields displayed. Select them one by one and move them with the arrow over to the list on the right.

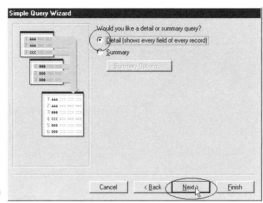

7 This is a detail query. A summary query would contain overall totals and similar.

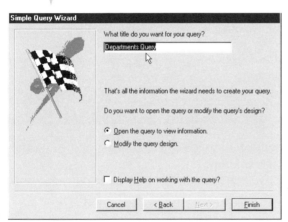

8 In the next step you are offered a query name. Overwrite the suggested name ...

What title do you want for your query?

| Employees' Birthdays |

9 ... with this name.

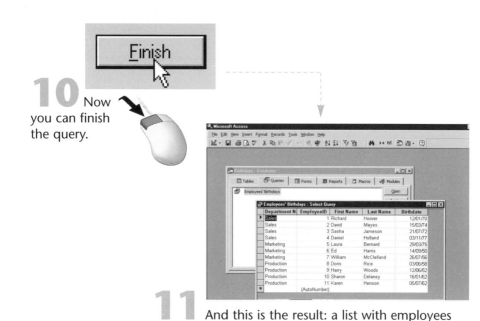

10 Now you can finish the query.

11 And this is the result: a list with employees and department names.

You can either print this table immediately or edit it further. Use the tools on the toolbar to sort and filter, or hide individual columns.

 You can use this tool to sort the records in descending order in the selected column.

 Use this tool to sort the records in ascending order.

 Clicking on this tool filters the records according to the selected criterion (e.g. department name).

 This tool allows you to generate a form in which you can enter the filter criterion for each column.

 This tool removes all the filters in the query.

 Click on this symbol to locate any record within the selected column(s).

The query remains stored in the Query module. If new records are entered in the tables, simply restart the query and it will include the new records.

Set up a further query, in this case a telephone list that contains only the last names of employees and their extension numbers. Start up the query wizard again and gather the fields from the two tables. Save the query as *Employees' Phone Numbers*.

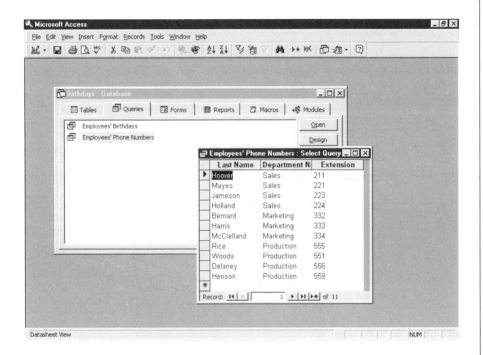

It is quite easy to change the places of the columns in the query output: just select the column by clicking on the column header, hold the mouse button down in this position and drag the column between two other columns.

Editing queries

In practice, queries set up using the Query Wizard are generally only the beginning. You really need to set up queries in the Query window, since this is the only way of ensuring you can make full use of all the possible ways of analysing the data. So set up and edit the next query in the Query window.

1 For the next query, switch to the Database window and select the Query tab. Click on *New*.

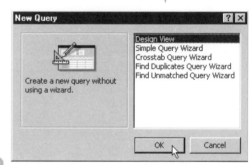

2 This time, select the Design View straight away.

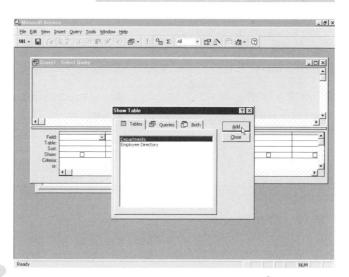

3 The query will be set up immediately. You will be offered all the tables from the Table module. Add the first one to the query.

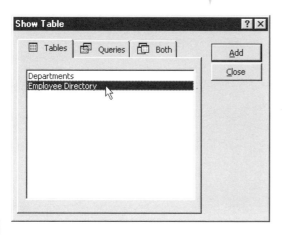

4 Select the second table..

5 ... and add this one as well.

201

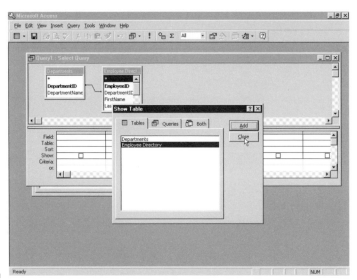

6 Now all the tables concerned with the query have been collected and you can close the list of tables.

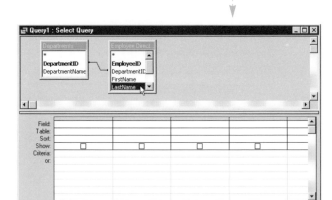

7 The first column is to contain last names. Select this field in the field list ...

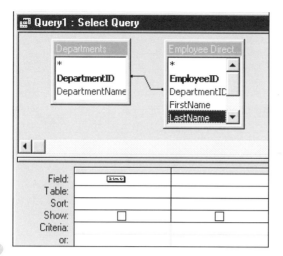

8 ... and, keeping the mouse button pressed down, drag it down into the query area.

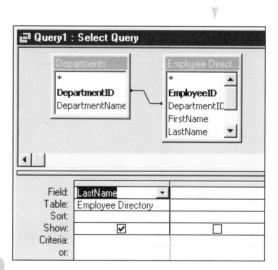

9 As soon as you release the mouse button, the field will be inserted.

203

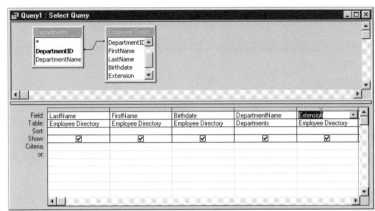

10 Drag down all the fields to the query area, in the same way, in the order you want them.

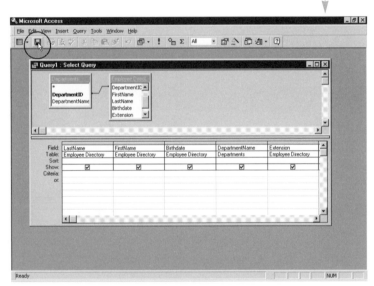

11 Now the query has been completed and you can save it, ...

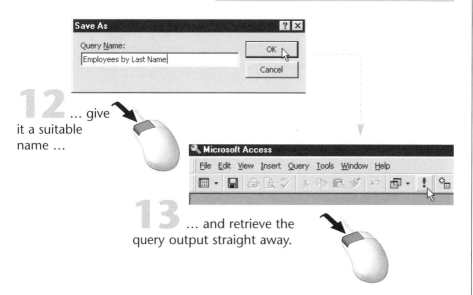

12 ... give
it a suitable
name ...

13 ... and retrieve the
query output straight away.

Here are a few useful techniques for setting up queries in the Design
window:

➤ You can transfer tables direct to a query from the Table
window by double-clicking with the mouse.

➤ To delete a table from a query, select it and press the `Delete`
key.

➤ If the query has already been set up, you can add new tables
using the menu command QUERY/SHOW TABLE.

Particularly long field lists can be imported into the query in no time by
double-clicking on the title row of the list. This automatically selects all the
fields and you can drag the selected block down with the mouse.

Sorting queries and hiding columns

You have already been shown above how to sort a query. But if you
want a query always to provide sorted data, you have to enter
details of the sorted field and the sort criteria into the query design.

You can take the opportunity to hide columns you don't need. This is particularly necessary when you need linked fields in the query but don't want to display them.

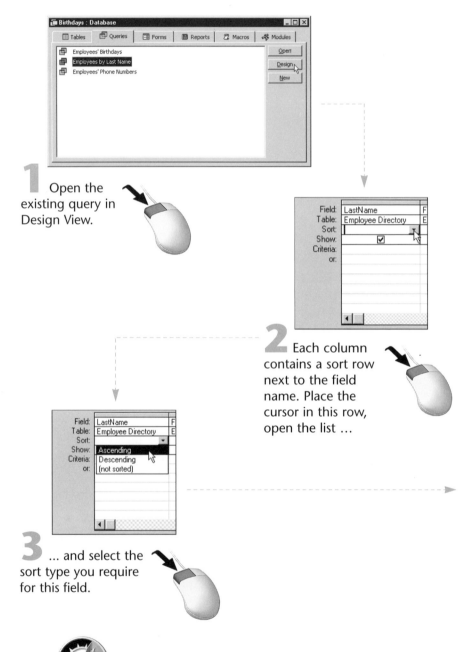

1 Open the existing query in Design View.

2 Each column contains a sort row next to the field name. Place the cursor in this row, open the list ...

3 ... and select the sort type you require for this field.

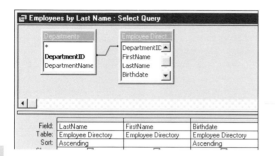

4 Now the query will be sorted according to the sort type in this field. You can enter further fields.

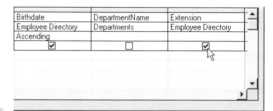

5 Remove the tick in the *Show* row if you want to hide a column.

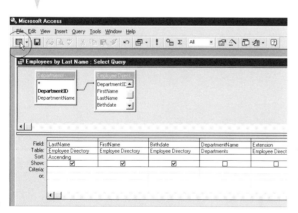

6 Clicking on this icon also allows you to view the query output.

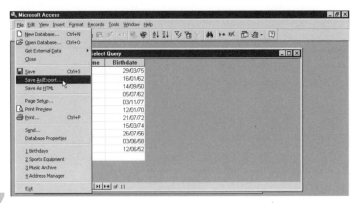

7 Resave the modified query under a new name using the FILE menu.

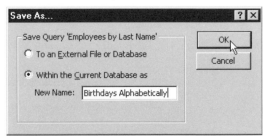

8 Enter the name of the new query here.

How are the **query fields sorted** if more than one sort field has been specified? The field that counts is the one furthest to the left. If this field contains more than one identical entry (e.g. identical last names), these are sorted again after the next field, etc.

Filtering queries with criteria

Another way of setting up queries is to use the *Criteria* row. This allows you to filter the query against the criteria you have specified. This may be a single-field entry, a department name for example, or it may also be a complex code.

Let's set up a query so that the output will contain only the employees in a particular department.

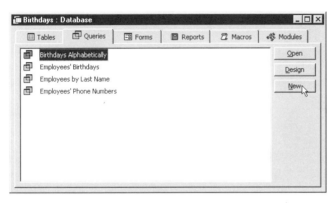

1 Start the next query in the Database window.

2 Select Design View again.

209

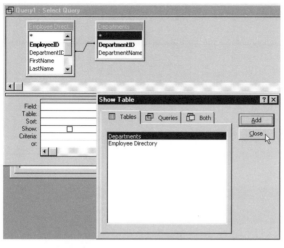

3 Add the two tables and close the Table window again.

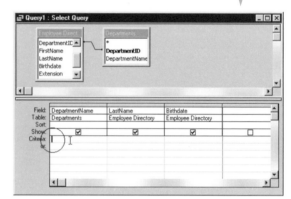

4 Move these three field names into the query and place the cursor in the Criteria row in the first column.

Field:	DepartmentName	LastName
Table:	Departments	Employee Directo
Sort:		
Show:	☑	☑
Criteria:	Sales	
or:		

5 Enter a department name.

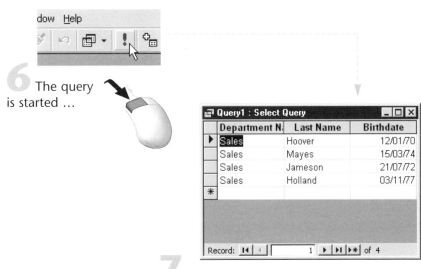

6 The query is started ...

7 ... and now presents only data records that fulfil this criterion.

You can use logical operators like *And* and *Or* in the criteria row, as well as *Between*, *Not* and *How*. Logical symbols such as >, = (greater than, equal to) are also allowed.

Here are a few examples of criteria for queries:

Field	Criterion	Meaning
Department	'Marketing' or 'Sales'	All records in which one of the departments appears
Department	Not 'Production'	All departments except Production
Last Name	As 'S*'	All names that begin with 'S'

Start your next query, which will be used as a basis for your monthly birthday report. This report lists the names of all employees who have birthdays in the current month.

211

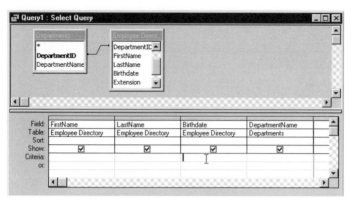

1 You can use a query that has already been set up or create a new query with these fields.

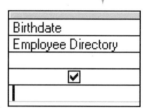

2 Place the cursor in the Criteria field in the birthday column.

3 Press ⬚ + F2 to open a zoom window in which you can enter the code.

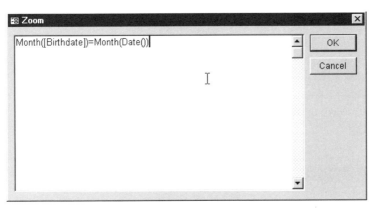

Enter this code. It compares the month of the date-of-birth field with that of the day's date.

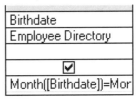

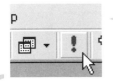

The code is transferred to the criteria field...

... and, when you start the query, ...

... the query displays only those employees who have a birthday in this month.

Save the query by clicking on the diskette icon on the toolbar using the name shown here.

The parameter query

You can also enter a criterion immediately before running a query. This is very convenient since it allows you, for example, to create a flexible department list in which you simply call up the department you require. You can also set up a birthday list for a particular month in this way.

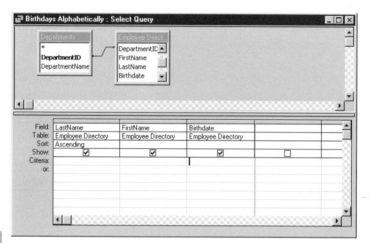

1 Call up the query that you have just set up and remove the code in the Criteria row.

FirstName	Birthdate	I
Employee Directory	Employee Directory	
☑	☑	☐

2 In the empty column beside the last field, enter the month of the date of birth. Press F2 to open the zoom window again.

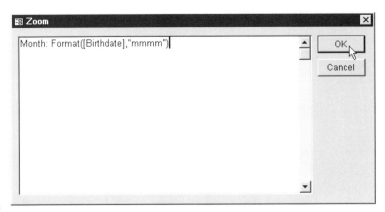

3 Enter this code, which will follow the *Format* instruction and calculate only the month of the *Date of Birth* field.

Field:	FirstName	Birthdate	Month: Format([Birth
Table:	Employee Directory	Employee Directory	
Sort:			
Show:	☑	☑	☑
Criteria:			[Which Month?]
or:			

4 In the Criteria row insert the question relating to the parameter query in square brackets.

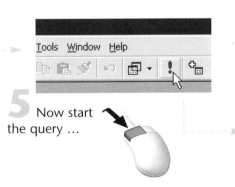

5 Now start the query …

215

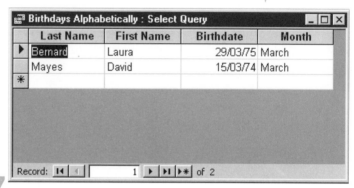

6 ... and enter the desired month.

7 Here is the result: the query filters the records according to the parameter you have entered.

> Don't forget to save the new query under a new name, using the menu command FILE/SAVE.

Quick progress check

Test your knowledge. This exercise will help you to refresh or reinforce what you have learned so far. Match the ten terms in the first table to the explanations below.

A   ⇧ + F2

B   Toolbox

C   OLE Object

D   As 'A*'

E   QUERY/DISPLAY TABLE

F   Parameter queries

G   Criterion

H   Activating sequence

I   Query

J   Sort

Match the terms to these possible answers:

1. This is the field data type for picture data (e.g. photos)

2. This is the toolbar which contains the combo box.

3. You need this option in the View menu to arrange form fields correctly.

4. If you need more than one table for a form, you have to create one of these.

5. You need this option in Query Design if a table is missing.

6. This is on the extreme left of the row in Query Design that puts the data records in alphabetical order.

7. This is what we specify in a query to filter the output.

8. With this criterion the query locates all fields that begin with A.

9. Press this when you want to see a code in the Zoom window.

10. This is the name for queries which ask in advance what they have to filter.

You'll find the answers in the appendix.

217

The shareware archive

What's in this chapter?

Issuing data records in reports is the central theme of this chapter. It is important for you to become familiar with the process of producing reports from a database. A report is quick to prepare with the aid of the Wizard and you will learn how to customise it for your own requirements. You can also use the report function for other purposes, for labels for instance. The examples here will show you how it's done. Also, to reinforce what you have already learned, you will again create a database with relationships and a query.

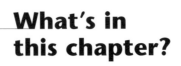

You already know:

You are going to learn:

Creating database tables

Like all the other examples in this book, this one involves a lot of work at the start. First, you need to design the database; this involves creating the tables and then establishing the relationships between them. We are going to create a shareware archive containing records of programs that employees will be able to borrow to try them out. To keep track of this, you need to set up a lending register containing details of the date on which the program is borrowed, the name of the program and the return date.

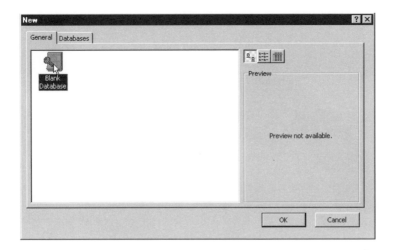

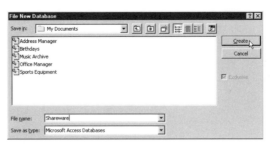

 Create a new MDB file using the menu command FILE/NEW DATABASE.

2 These are the tables in the Table module that we need for the model database. You can now begin your shareware archive.

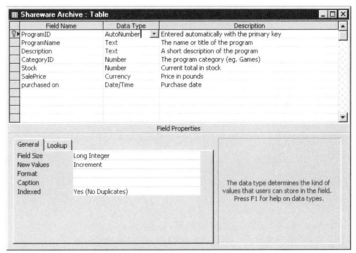

3 Build a link for the category; the other fields are standard.

4 Here are the next files. You can copy them from the database you created in the previous chapter (see below).

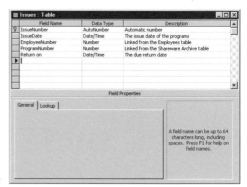

5 And this is the lending table that contains linking fields to the employee table and the shareware archive.

It's easy to copy the tables from the existing databases: open the database with the table, select it in the Table module and select the menu command EDIT/COPY. Then switch to the new database, select the Table module again and retrieve the table using menu command EDIT/PASTE. Now all you have to do is enter a table name and confirm that you want to transfer the structure and the data.

Relational links

Now, the tables have to be linked together. To do this a link line is dragged from each window which contains a primary key field to the field reserved for it in the other table.

And that's literally what happens; the links are built up like this in the Relationships window.

1 Open the Relationships window from the TOOLS menu.

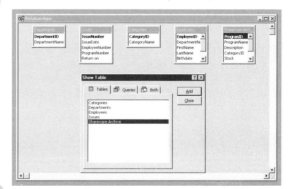

2 Insert all the tables from the Table module into the window. Double-clicking on an item will transfer it immediately to the window.

223

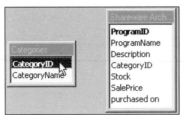

3 Now build the relationship between categories and the shareware archive. Point to the primary key field.

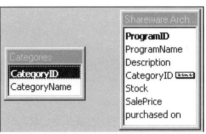

4 With the mouse button pressed down, drag it into the shareware archive table. Release the mouse button when the field is positioned over the linked field with the same name.

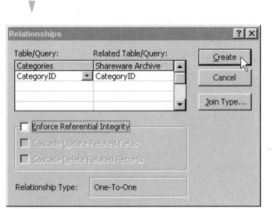

5 The linked field appears. Confirm the relationship.

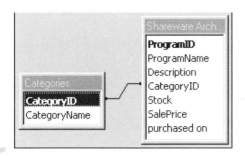

6 The result: a line links the two tables to display the relationship between them.

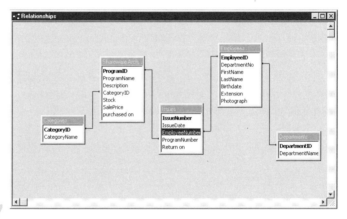

7 And this is what the network of relationships looks like once all the link lines are drawn.

All that's missing now are the data in the individual tables. You can record these in the data sheets, or you can use forms which you create as AutoForms, including combo boxes for the linked data fields. The category list contains a series of shareware categories:

- Games
- Utilities
- System Tools
- Graphics/CAD
- Languages
- Office Software
- Finance
- Music/Video
- Internet/Intranet

Here are a few test data for the shareware archive (you can fill in the remaining columns as you like):

Program name	Brief description
Translator XXX	Translation program
AllFinance	Loan interest calculation
DisC-Play	Music & CD manager
Graphics Texture Collection	Textures for designers
HTML Light	HTML editor with tag colouring
Internet Phone	Live talk for the Internet
Conquistador	Historical action game
Paint Shop Pro	Graphics and photo-editing
Monster Truck	Action game
Picture Publisher	DTP program
Quotations & Sayings	Dictionary of quotes and sayings

Setting up queries for the program list

To produce a report that contains all the programs in the shareware archive, you need to set up a query. The *Shareware Archive* table alone does not provide you with sufficient information since it contains only the category numbers and not the category descriptions for the individual items.

1 In the Database window click on the Query module and create a new query.

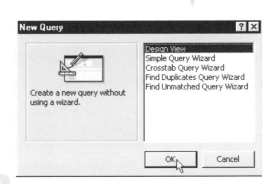

2 It's quickest to work in Design View.

227

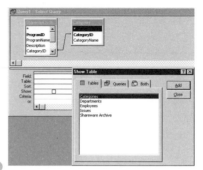

3 Insert the Shareware Archive table and the categories table into the query by double-clicking and close the table window.

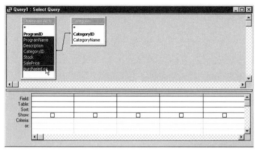

4 Select the fields from the first table one after the other, by keeping the ⓪ key pressed.

5 Move the selected fields down to the first column ...

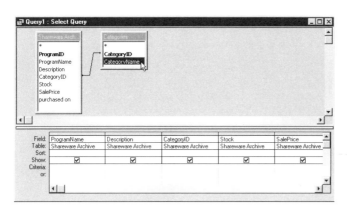

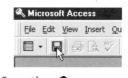

6 ...and then release the mouse button. The fields from the first table are now in the query. Retrieve the Category description field from the second table by double-clicking and place it in the last column.

7 Save the query ...

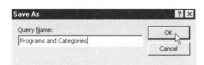

8 ... and enter a name for it.

9 The result: a first query in the Query module in the Database window.

229

The first report: A program list

Now it's time for the first report, which will include a list of the shareware items from the database. We have already set up the query, which contains not only the programs but the categories, so you can start right away:

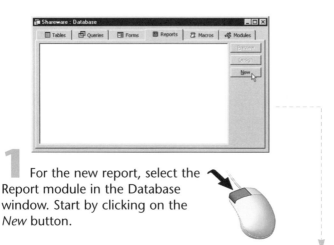

1 For the new report, select the Report module in the Database window. Start by clicking on the *New* button.

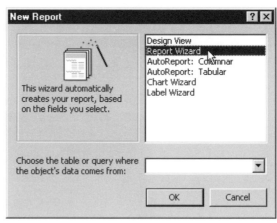

2 Select the Report Wizard. This will talk you through to the finished report.

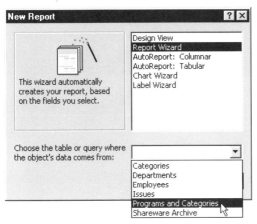

3 In the bottom right of the window, select the table or query from which the report is to be created. Click on the small black triangle ...

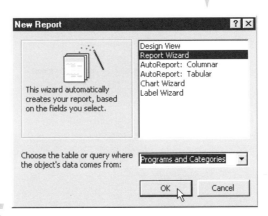

4 ... and select the query you created before.

5 Press *OK* to go on to the next step.

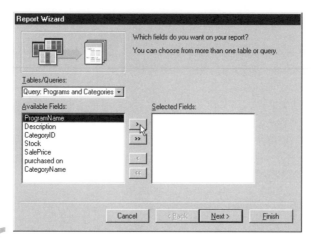

6 Select the fields which the report is to contain. Highlight the first field and click on the arrow.

The list will automatically contain all the tables and also the queries. But you can't see whether an entry refers to a table or a query. If you are not sure, open the Database window in the background and look up in the individual modules.

Once the data source has been selected, you will be offered all the fields contained in it and you can collect together the fields you need for the report.

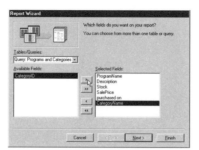

1 Click on the arrow icon to move all fields except for the *CategoryID* over to the right-hand list.

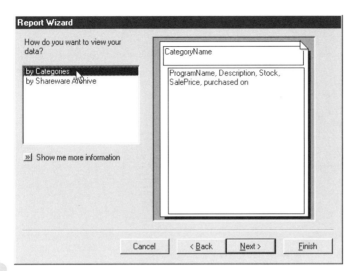

2 In the next step you will be asked to specify the grouping field for the report. Select grouping by Categories.

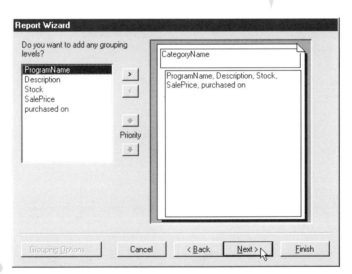

3 The preview shows how the category will be inserted as a group, and now you can move on to the next step.

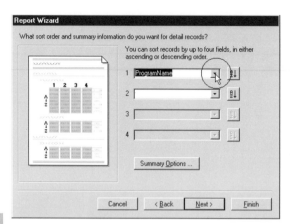

4 Specify an ascending sort for the program description field.

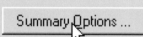

5 The Summary Options button gives you options for report totals and summary options.

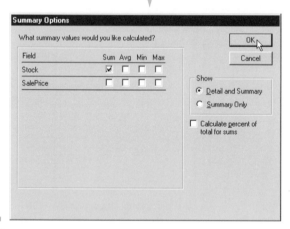

6 Specify that you want to calculate stock totals for the individual categories.

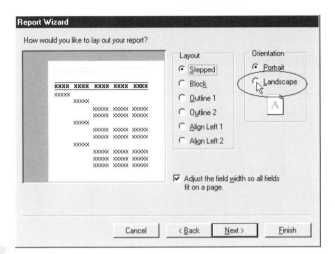

7 In the layout window select the Landscape option.

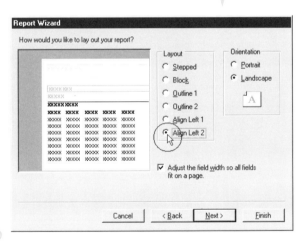

8 Choose a space-saving layout with left alignment.

235

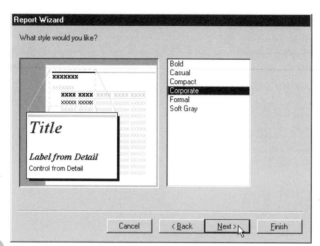

9 The styling sets the colours, font types and sizes and line elements of the report.

10 Now give your report a name ...

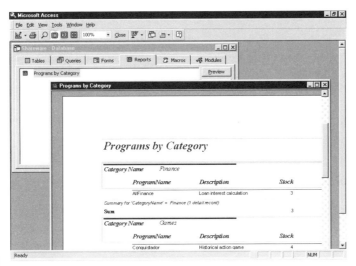

11 ... and after a brief pause, you will receive a program list with groupings and subtotals.

To take a good look at the report, use the *Zoom Lens* and *Zoom Field*:

Zoom Lens: zooms between the selected zoom and full page view.

Zoom Field: select the zoom factor that fits your screen.

Now you can use the Report Wizard to set up other reports, perhaps a list of employees according to departments or a program list sorted according to purchase price.

Designing reports

You can, of course, design your report yourself in Design mode, doing everything from setting up pages and individual fields to drawing elements such as lines. Let's start on our first report and edit it directly in Design mode.

1 Select the report in the Reports module in the Database window ...

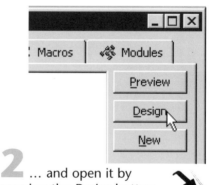

2 ... and open it by pressing the *Design* button.

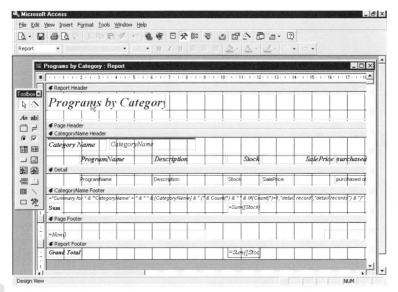

3 This is what the design looks like. Reports, like forms, are divided up into areas. If, for example, you select the title element in the report header ...

4 ... you can read its formatting on the toolbar and modify it if you want to (in this case, cancel the italics).

Have a look at the VIEW menu. This contains the most important elements: the Page Header/Footer and Report Header/Footer. By clicking on them you can reveal or hide them.

In the Header and Detail area you will need formatting (font, colours, italics, bold, etc.) not just for individual elements but for the whole row. Learn how to select whole rows:

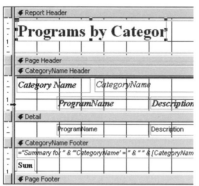

1 To select a whole row of elements, point to the line edge. The mouse cursor will become an arrow.

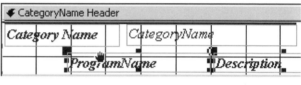

2 A click selects all the elements in this row.

3 Push the elements in the Detail area up to the top edge …

4 …and drag the bottom edge of the area upwards so that there is no wasted space between the rows.

Codes in reports

If you scroll the vertical scroll bar to the right and the horizontal scroll bar downwards, you can see the page number code at the bottom in the Page Footer. Similar codes can be incorporated in every area; you just need a text box which you draw using the appropriate tool from the toolbox. This is how you find out where the code is and what it looks like:

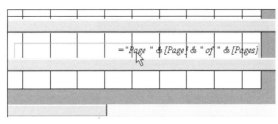

1 Double-click on the text box containing the code to select it. This will open the Properties window.

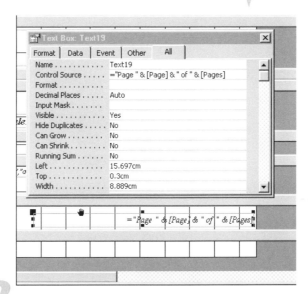

2 You will see that the code is located under *Control Source*.

Program

Text Box: Text2

| Format | Data | Event | Other | All |

Name Text2
Control Source . . . . . ="Summary for " & "'CategoryName' = "
Format . . . .
Decimal Places . . . . . Auto
Input Mask . . . .
Visible . . . . Yes
Hide Duplicates . . . . . No
Can Grow . . . . No
Can Shrink . . . . No
Running Sum . . . . . . No
Left 0.101cm
Top 0cm
Width 24.49cm

CategoryName Footer

="Summary for " & "'CategoryName' = " & " " & " " & [CategoryName] & " (" & Count(*) & " "

Sum   =Sum(

Page Footer

=Now()

3 Here is a slightly more complicated
code to summarise the category totals.

In order to be able to edit
the codes more easily, place
the cursor in the property
field and press `⇧` + `F2`.
The Zoom window now
gives you more space for
longer codes.

Where is the information about
grouping levels and sorting
stored? You will find this
information in a separate
window, and if you want to, you
can delete different groups here
or add new ones.

| View | Insert | Format | Tools |

- Design View
- Layout Preview
- Print Preview

- Properties
- Field List
- Sorting and Grouping
- Code

- ✓ Ruler
- ✓ Grid
- ✗ Toolbox

- ✓ Page Header/Footer
- ✓ Report Header/Footer

- Toolbars ▶

1 Call up the SORTING AND GROUPING
command in the VIEW menu.

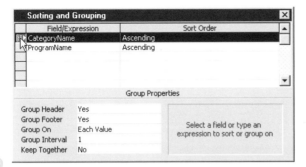

2 The window displays all grouping and sorting options, with each row representing a group or a sort.

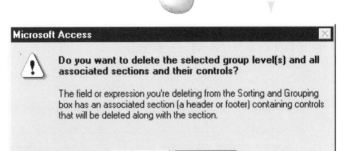

3 If you mark a row and delete it using the `Delete` key, you will receive a warning that you will also lose the elements in this group.

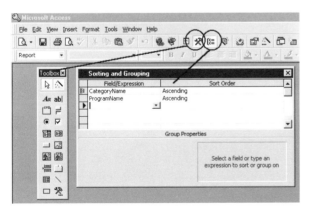

There are two icons on the toolbar that you can use to switch the toolbox and the *Sorting and Grouping* window on and off.

243

Assigning AutoFormat

You can reformat an area of your report not just by selecting individual elements but by assigning it an AutoFormat. AutoFormats are the report styles that the Report Wizard suggests shortly before the report is completed. If you want to format a particular area differently, simply assign it a new AutoFormat.

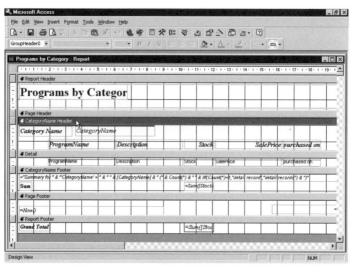

1 Select the area you want to format by clicking on the relevant row.

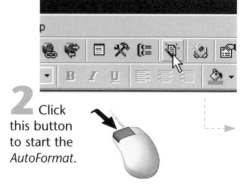

2 Click this button to start the AutoFormat.

3 The list of ready-made report styles will be displayed again. Select the format you want.

4 The options also give you the possibility of removing attributes. If, for example, you remove the tick beside Font, this attribute will not be changed by the AutoFormat.

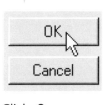

5 Click the *OK* button ...

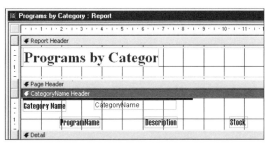

6 ... and this area of your report will be automatically formatted in the new style.

Using a report to create labels

The single-column report is the most common, but not the only type of report used in practice. You will frequently be required to print reports in table form or on preprinted forms. You will also need to create a report if you want to print labels, and you will discover that Access recognises not only this type of report but most label sizes as well.

1 Start the next report again in the Report module in the Database window.

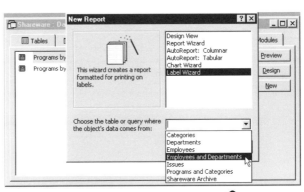

2 Switch to the Label Wizard and select the query that contains employees and department names.

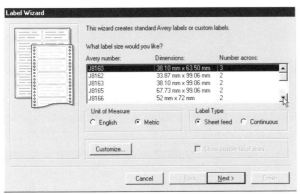

3 In the next window you will be shown a list of label formats. Scroll through with the scroll bar until you have found the right format, ...

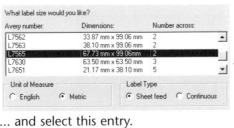

4 ... and select this entry.

247

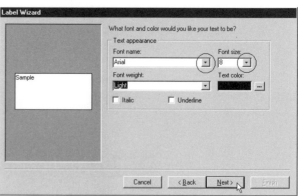

5 Once you have selected the label size, the Wizard will take you on to the next step.

6 You will be asked to specify the font size and font type for the label, as well as the font weight and colour.

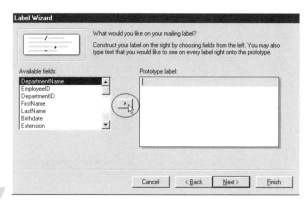

7 You can now assemble the fields from the query that you want to appear on the label. Start with the first name.

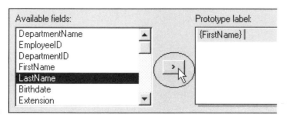

8 Press the space key and add the last name to the label.

9 To move to the next line, press the ⏎ key.

249

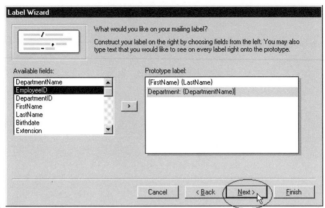

10 You can also enter text before adding the field. Then finish designing your label.

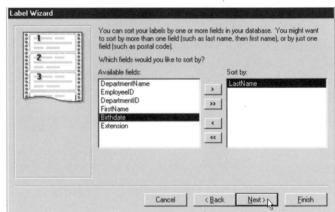

11 In the next query, move the field to the right column for sorting.

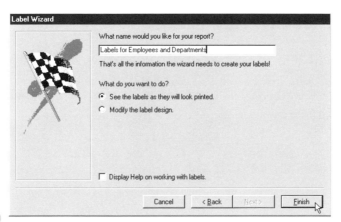

 Give your
report an appropriate
name and finish it.

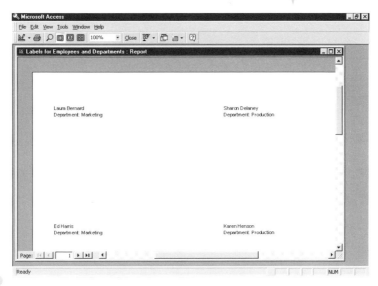

The result: the individual records are
printed on the labels in the selected format.

Quick progress check

Do you know how to do it now? Test yourself with this revision exercise. Simply put a cross beside the answer you think comes closest to the truth. You will find the answers in the appendix (but test yourself first!).

1. To copy a table from one database to another ...	a) the first database has to be deleted b) use the Copy and Paste commands from the Edit menu c) copy the table in an Excel window
2. You can also create links in the Relationship window ...	a) by overlaying field lists b) with the line tool from the Toolbox c) by using the mouse to drag the first field to the second
3. To create a report you will need ...	a) a table or a query b) at least three days c) a form
4. The report style determines ...	a) the paper size for the report b) the font type and size and the line elements in the report c) who is entitled to have access to the report
5. The report title generally ...	a) is positioned in the detail area b) is positioned in the Report Header c) bears no relation to the report

6. Complete rows of elements ...

a) cannot be selected at all

b) do not occur at all

c) can be selected by clicking the mouse pointer at the left edge of the row

7. The page number is generally positioned ...

a) as a code in the Page Footer

b) on a completely different page

c) as a code in the Report Footer

8. You can read what fields are included in the grouping in ...

a) View/Filter

b) View/Sorting and Grouping

c) the detail records of the report

9. AutoFormat changes ...

a) the style of the report

b) the paper size of the report

c) the table settings

10. The label size of a label report ...

a) cannot be changed

b) can be selected from a wide range of options or designed by you

c) depends on the paper size of the report

You'll find the answers in the appendix.

8

Holiday offers

What's in
this chapter?

You are about to learn a number of more
advanced techniques for dealing with forms.
You can make your forms considerably more
useful, for example, by using subforms. For
revision purposes you will again be asked to
create tables and relationships and set up
queries for your practical database.

You already know:

You are going to learn:

Model table

You run a travel agency and, as a proficient Access user, you naturally want to use your database program to help you manage your business activities. These include

- creating a list of holiday offers

- recording customer data

- recording records of completed holidays

To create a useful database, we need a table model with relationships established between the individual data sets. Start by creating a new database.

1 After starting Access, choose the first option from the selection window ...

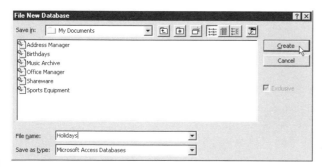

2 ... and give the new database the name
Holidays. The MDB suffix will identify the file as
an Access database.

3 These are the tables you need to create in
the Table module. Begin with the customer table.

This shows you all the field structures for the different tables:

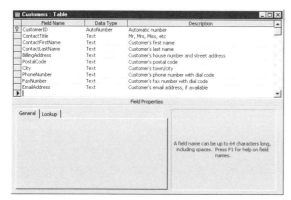

The customer table will
include the customers'
details including full
address, telephone
number, and – for
holidays offered on the
Internet – email address.
Data on holidays offers
or bookings do not
belong in the customer
table. You will create
another table for these.

257

Enter the following test data (you can fill in the remaining fields as you like):

Customer No	Title	First name	Last Name	Street	Town	Postcode
1	Mr	John	Starr	32 Parkside Close	Bristol	BR4 3RL
2	Mrs	Margaret	Harrison	14 Victoria Gardens	Bath	BA2 5TN
3	Mrs	Caroline	Stepford	97 Woodland Grove	Gloucester	GL1 8PF
4	Dr	George	Morgan	5 Kipling Avenue	Bristol	BR3 6GY
5	Mrs	Tracy	Clements	189 Clifton Road	Cambridge	CB2 5PT
6	Dr	Philip	Harrod	76 Churchill Street	Bath	BA1 9JT
7	Mr	Martin	Kirby	84 Brookfield Road	Bristol	BR3 8GS
8	Miss	Janet	Cousins	65 Rossiter Street	Cardiff	CA2 6GR

TIP

Hot tip: What do you do if the customer numbers in the AutoNumber field are no longer in ascending order because you have deleted a wrong entry or sorted the records? It's quite simple. Switch to Table Design. Remove the primary key from the field, delete the field and insert it again immediately with AutoNumber as the data type and the primary key. Now all the records will be numbered in ascending order again.

Here is the table with the holiday offers. It contains the holiday name as it is described in the brochure, the price, and dates of arrival/departure.
Set up the 'Destination Country' field as a number field set to *Long Integer.* We will store the countries in a separate table to avoid data redundancy.

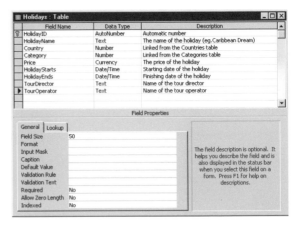

As an alternative you can also link the Tour Operator field to an external list with the names of the tour operators.

WHAT'S THIS? Data redundancy occurs when the same data have to be recorded and saved several times.

Here are some specimen data for this table.

Holiday	Destination country	Category	Price	Begin	End	Tour director	Tour operator
Caribbean Dream	6	1	£ 882	14.6.98	14.6.98	Jones	Dream Tours
Scenic Mallorca	2	1	£ 379	12.5.98	19.5.98	Jones	Iberia Travel
Greek Wine	4	1	£ 432	1.4.98	9.4.98	Hill	TUWI
Florence by Night	1	5	£ 279	14.3.98	21.3.98	Hill	TUWI

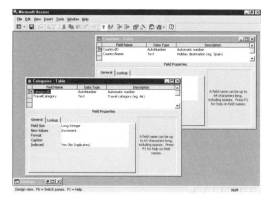

These are the two tables to which the holiday list will be related. The *Category* field stores the holiday category, the field with the destination countries contains the names of the countries, and you could also add further fields (airport, comments, etc.).

Category no.	Category
1	Air
2	Rail
3	Sea
4	Coach
5	Car

Destination country no.	Destination country
1	Italy
2	Spain
3	Turkey
4	Greece
5	USA
6	Dom. Republic

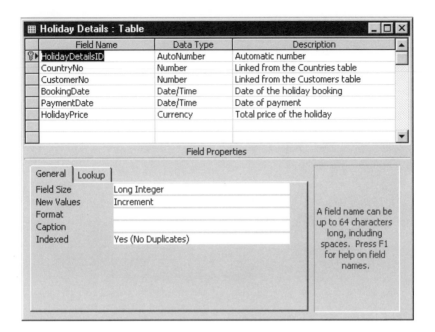

Field Name	Data Type	Description
HolidayDetailsID	AutoNumber	Automatic number
CountryNo	Number	Linked from the Countries table
CustomerNo	Number	Linked from the Customers table
BookingDate	Date/Time	Date of the holiday booking
PaymentDate	Date/Time	Date of payment
HolidayPrice	Currency	Total price of the holiday

Field Properties

General | Lookup

Field Size	Long Integer
New Values	Increment
Format	
Caption	
Indexed	Yes (No Duplicates)

A field name can be up to 64 characters long, including spaces. Press F1 for help on field names.

Finally, the most important table, the *Holiday Details*. Since you cannot store any 'transaction data' (bookings, processed holidays) either in the table with the customer data or in the holiday offers table, you need to create a further table that refers back to these two data files via linking fields. This table stores the records of the bookings of the individual customers. Record the booking date (important for holiday cancellations) and the payment date, and also create a field for the holiday price actually paid. This amount will generally differ from the price stored in the holiday offers because of discounts, refunds, etc.

Relationships

Build up the relationships in the Relationship window as you were shown in the previous chapter, by dragging a link line from the primary key field in one table to the linked field in the other table.

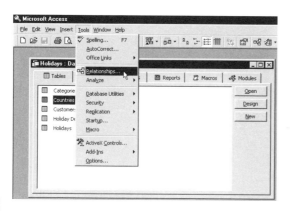

1 Start by selecting TOOLS/ RELATIONSHIPS.

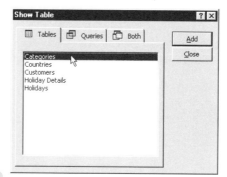

2 Add all the tables by simply double-clicking on the table names.

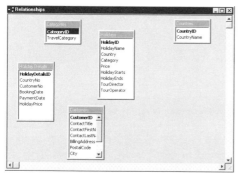

3 Arrange the individual field lists in a logical order by dragging the mouse pointer in the title bar.

261

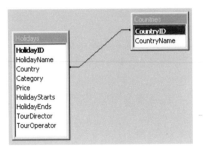

4 Drag the first link line between Holidays and Countries.

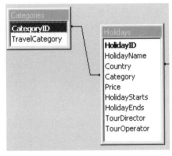

5 Then create a link to the Categories table.

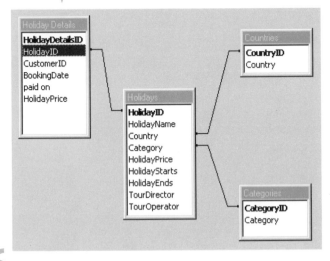

6 Now link up the *HolidayID* in the *Holiday Details* table to the Holidays table.

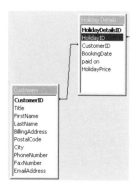

7 All that remains is to link the Customer Number to the *Holiday Details* table ...

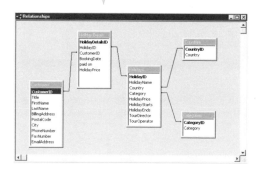

8 ... and the relationships in your relational database are now perfect.

9 Save the layout and close it.

In practice you will find that relationships prevent you from performing other actions in the database, for example, changing the field data type or re-organizing fields in tables. In this case you will have to delete the relationships briefly, perform the action and restore the relationships. To delete a relationship, call up TOOLS/RELATIONSHIPS from the main menu, highlight the relationship line between the tables and simply press the Delete key.

263

Creating forms

To record data in the individual tables, you can initially create AutoForms. Just highlight the table names in the Table Module and press the AutoForm function on the toolbar. AutoForms are created without dialog. Just save them under a form name.

But our complex network of database relationships needs more convenient input masks. You have already learned in the previous chapter how you provide access to the list of destination countries in the holiday table:

1 Start with an AutoForm for the holiday table.

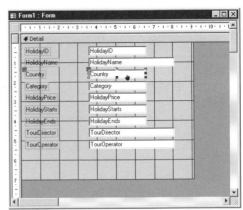

2 Switch directly to Design mode and delete the destination country field since it relates only to the destination country number.

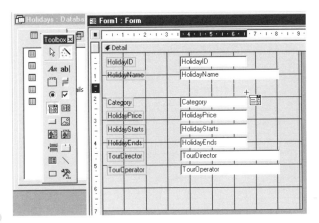

3 Using the combo box tool from the toolbox, insert a new field.

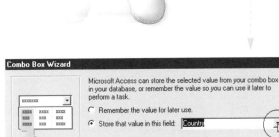

4 Answer the Wizard's questions, bring the name of the destination country into the field and link it to the field in the holiday list.

265

5 The combination field is complete. Now create the field for the travel category in the same way.

If it is not displayed, you can **activate the toolbox** by clicking a button on the toolbar. If no wizard starts for the production of a combination field, you can activate it by clicking the tool in the top right of the toolbox.

Form formatting

As practical as they are, the AutoForms do not look good. Here are some form designing techniques:

➡ Drag the bottom right corner of the form section to enlarge the form.

➡ Open a new section for the title by using the menu command VIEW/FORM HEADER/FOOTER. Draw in a designation element and type in the heading *Holiday Offers*.

➡ Select all the active fields in the left-hand part of the form and click on the menu command FORMAT/ALIGNMENT/RIGHT.

➡ Drag the mouse across all the active and text fields and click the menu command FORMAT/VERTICAL SPACING/INCREASE twice.

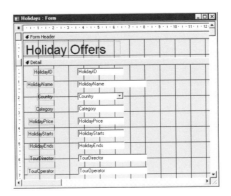

Ctrl + A
also selects all
the elements
in the form.

The 'Holiday Bookings' form

You enter the bookings for the individual holidays in the *Holiday Details* table, because here you provided the customer number and the number of the holiday as linked fields. You could again create a form for this table, delete the elements provided for the number fields and include combination fields for the list of customers and the list of holiday offers.

But there is another way: change the structure of the table so that it already 'knows' where the customer data and the holiday offers are coming from. If you then create a form from the table, it will automatically have the appropriate combination fields.

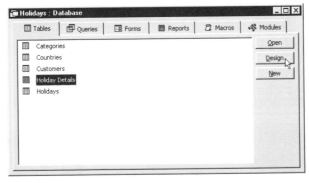

Open the *Holiday Details* table in Design view.

267

Holiday Details : Table		
Field Name	Data Type	Description
HolidayDetailsID	AutoNumber	Automatic number
HolidayID	Number	Connected to the Holidays table
CustomerID	Number	Connected to the Customers table
BookingDate	Date/Time	Date of the booking
paid on	Date/Time	Date of payment
HolidayPrice	Currency	Price of the holiday in pounds

2 Select the number field
linked to the *HolidayID*. ...

Holiday Details : Table		
Field Name	Data Type	
HolidayDetailsID	AutoNumber	Automatic number
HolidayID	Number	Connected to the Holidays table
CustomerID	Text	Connected to the Customers table
BookingDate	Memo	Date of the booking
paid on	Number	Date of payment
HolidayPrice	Date/Time	Price of the holiday in pounds
	Currency	
	AutoNumber	
	Yes/No	
	OLE Object	
	Hyperlink	
	Lookup Wizard...	

3 ... and from the data type list,
click on the Lookup Wizard.

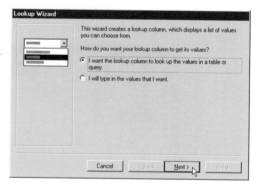

Lookup Wizard

This wizard creates a lookup column, which displays a list of values you can choose from.

How do you want your lookup column to get its values?

○ I want the lookup column to look up the values in a table or query.

○ I will type in the values that I want.

Cancel   < Back   Next >   Finish

4 You can confirm the
first option as suggested.

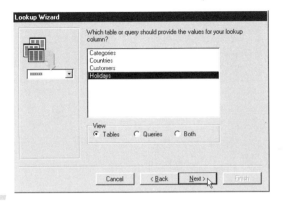

5 *Holidays* is the table that supplies the data to the field.

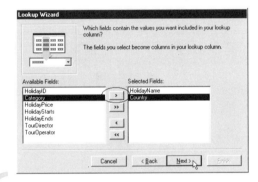

6 Take these fields from the other table.

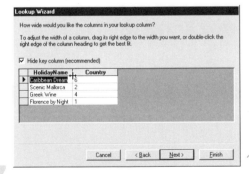

7 You can make the large description field slightly wider by dragging.

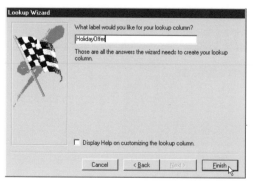

8 All that remains is the new column heading for the field ...

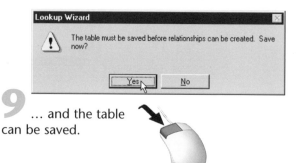

9 ... and the table can be saved.

The table has now been prepared so that, instead of the number, the two fields from the holidays table are automatically integrated into forms, into tables and into datasheets. We now need to adopt the same procedure for the field with the *CustomerID*, because it too comes from a different table:

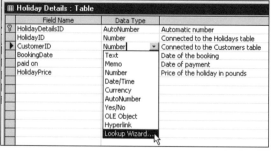

1 Start the Lookup Wizard for this field again.

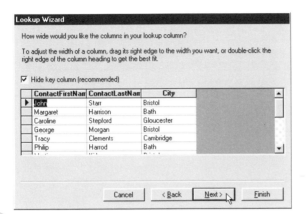

Use the customers table as data supplier and take these three fields.

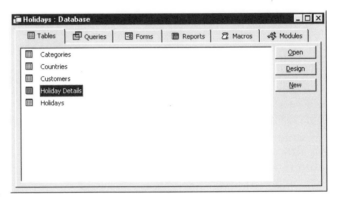

Confirm the remaining options. Save and close the design of this table.

Now you can make an AutoForm for this table. This will create a relationship not only with the *Holiday Details* table, but also with the *Customers* and *Holidays* tables.

1 Select the table in the tables module. Start the AutoForm using the button on the toolbar.

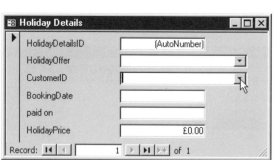

2 And that's it. You now have a fully functional form for holiday bookings. The combination fields, such as the customer field here …

3 … integrate the data entered in the other tables automatically.

Forms and subforms

The facility that a form has to work with combination fields supplying data from other, linked tables makes the database highly flexible, and if you build on the help of the Wizard you will not go far wrong. The combination fields do have one drawback however: they cannot accept data and save it in their base tables. In practice, this means that while you can book holidays with a form, you cannot simultaneously modify customer data or holiday offers.

For such purposes you need subforms. The subform is embedded in a form as an object. It displays the data from another table and, if you wish, prepares it for alteration.

Prerequisite: Query

For forms based on several databases, you will need a query to integrate the data. Create a query for the holiday offers and details:

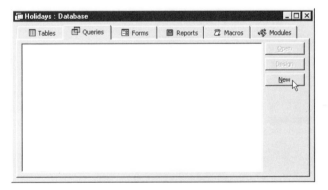

Click on the query tab in the database window and then on *New*.

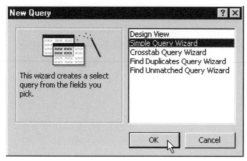

2 A wizard is again helpfully to hand.

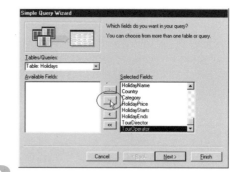

3 Start with the *Holidays* table, and from it place all the fields onto the field list.

4 From the *Holiday Details* table, you need the following fields: *CustomerID*, *BookingDate*, *paid on* and *HolidayPrice* (actually paid, different from the first price, the offer price).

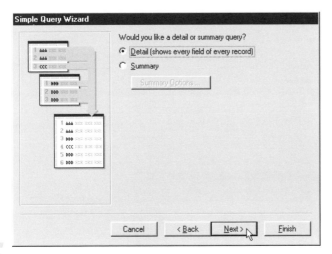

5 Confirm the next option, we want to see the details, …

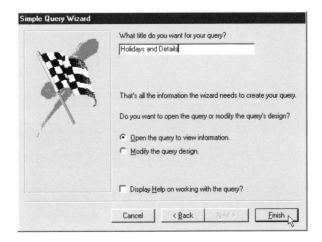

6 … and save the query under this name.

Then you can look at the query once more in Query Design view and close the window.

275

The subform

You must enter the
customer data separately,
which can also be done
using the subform
(though we don't want
to overstate the case).

To include the holiday bookings, we
shall now create a combination of form
and subform. This form will allow you
to include new holiday offers and the
booking data for them simultaneously.

1 Click on the forms tab
and start with the design
of a new form.

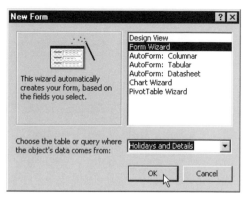

2 The Form Wizard will
again help you. From the list
at the bottom, click on the
query you have just created.

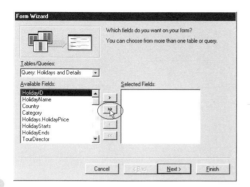

3 You selected the fields carefully in the query so that you can retrieve the list in full.

Click Next to go to the next dialog box ...

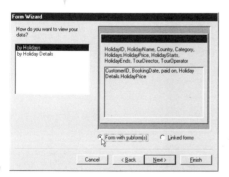

5 ... in which you determine the breakdown between main form and subform. In our case the data is displayed by holidays, so the holiday offers constitute the main form.

277

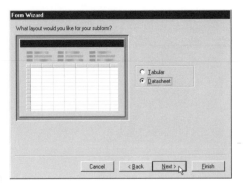

6 The next step is to set the layout for the subform. The Datasheet View is best here, but you could also display the table.

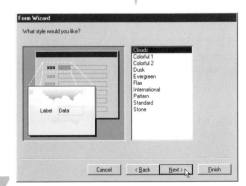

7 Here you choose a style, which determines background, font and font size …

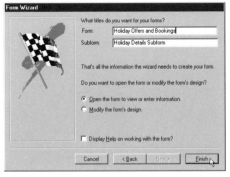

8 … and then you can name the form. As a subform is to be saved at the same time, this too requires a name.

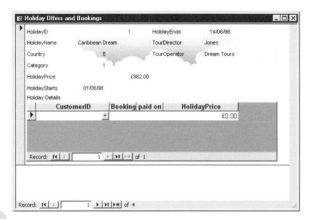

And this is the result. The main form shows the holiday offers from the *Holidays* table, while you can use the subform to enter the holiday bookings, which are consequently saved in *Holiday Details*.

Note the two sets of navigation buttons at the bottom left of the form. The arrows on the inside refer to the subform, and on the form edge you have the navigation buttons for the records of the main form.

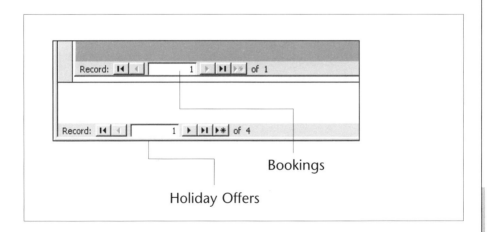

Bookings

Holiday Offers

279

Now include the data with this form, enter bookings for the holiday offers, select the customers in the subform and enter the booking data.

The Wizard suggests another combination, that is two forms linked to one another. This would be an alternative to the subform. Simply place these two forms next to one another and edit them simultaneously.

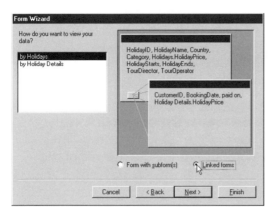

You can edit the subform like any other form. Activate it on the forms tab of the database window, change column widths, font and line spacing and save the form again. If you open the main form, the subform is only indicated as an object. But you can determine the size of the form in it.

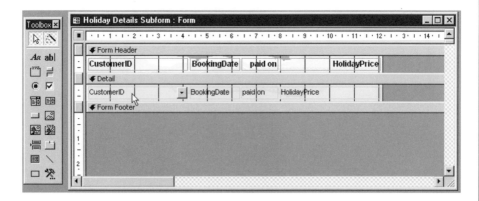

Quick progress check

Fill in the gaps with the correct terms:

The fields in a table structure that are linked to fields in other tables must be of the ——————— (1) field data type. The size of these fields is given by ——————— (2). Relationships between the tables can be viewed and changed under Tools ——————— (3). To create a relationship the ——————— (4) of one table is dragged to the linked field of the other table. You can delete a selected relationship line with the ——————— (5) key. You can justify form elements by way of the ——————— (6) menu. You can increase the vertical spacing with the ——————— (7) option from this menu. A subform makes the data from a ——————— (8) table or query available for editing. If there is a subform in the main form, ——————— (9) different navigation buttons can be seen. The outer arrows control the records in the ——————— (10).

You'll find the answers in the appendix.

Invoices

What's in
this chapter?

If, up to now, you have been using a word
processing program for your invoices, then you
won't have very much automation in your
databases. You cannot do more than insert a
recipient file by way of the form letter function.
In this chapter you will learn about how Access
tackles such tasks. And you will discover how to
convert Access data into Excel tables or make
them available
to Word and
you will
acquire a
knowledge
of data
protection.

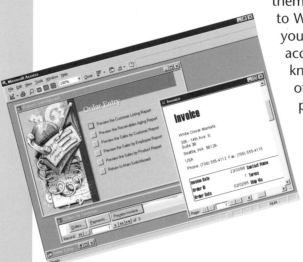

You already know:

You are going to learn:

283

Order processing

Anyone who has had anything to do with invoicing programs will know the problem: invoicing is more than simply inserting a sheet of paper, typing the customer's address, listing the items and calculating the total plus value added tax, and then entering the figure at the bottom.

If you require some level of organisation in your work, you can use Access to set up an order processing routine that incorporates automatic invoicing. The invoice then becomes a function of the records in the order table and is linked to the customer and item data.

In previous chapters you had ample opportunity to use Access to practise with relationships and relational links. In every case Access puts helpful wizards at your disposal.

We are now going to introduce a wizard that can create a complete database for order processing with integrated invoicing. You can easily modify this database to suit your own requirements.

Creating databases

Once Access has started, you will see a list of the databases created so far. Switch to the *Database Wizard* option.

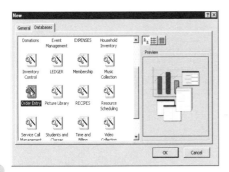

Here you will
see all the wizards
available to choose
from. The wizard
we need is called
Order, so select
it …

… and
start it by
clicking OK.

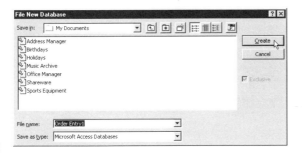

A name for the
database is suggested;
either accept it …

File name: Order Entry

… or enter a
name of your own …

285

6 ... and confirm it.

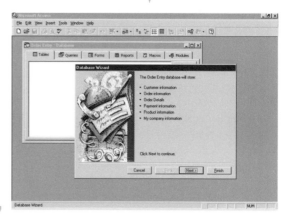

7 This message tells you everything the wizard is going to create.

8 Confirm this dialog field as well ...

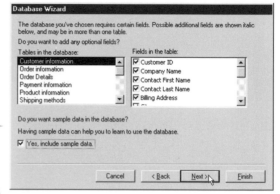

9 ... and the wizard will display the tables with field lists.

Remember that some of the fields serve as key fields for the links. It is better to leave all the fields in the tables. You can always remove them later in table design.

These field lists are only suggestions, of course. You do not have to accept any of the fields. Simply remove the check mark in front of the fields that you do not need in your database. You can click on the italicised fields and so incorporate them into the tables as well.

The example

☑ Yes, include sample data.

data will help you to test out the tables, so be sure to check this option.

Next, the wizard will want to know what style you intend to apply to your screens. This means the background, along with the fonts and font sizes in the forms. Be sure to keep them simple, because otherwise you will only upset the time-consuming formatting when it comes to editing the form elements.

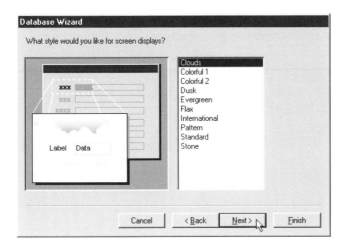

The same goes for the reports: keep them simple and compact so that they do not take up too much room and are easier to edit.

287

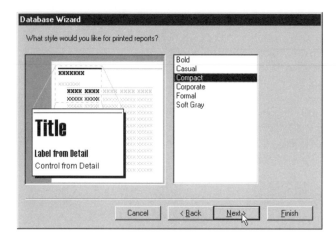

Now, all that the wizard needs to know is what the new database is going to be called. By this we mean the forms and reports; you entered the name of the database file earlier on. Once you have confirmed one last message, the database will be created which, depending on the power of your computer, may take several minutes.

Then you will see the switchboard window displayed, with the database window reduced to icon size and placed bottom left.

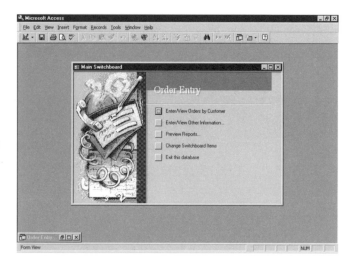

Where is this switchboard (which is nothing more than a standard form) located? How does Access know which form to display on opening the database? You can do this automatically by way of the menu command TOOLS/STARTUP. This is where you will find the list of all forms and you can designate one of them as your switchboard.

Relationships

The most important thing about a relational database is, of course, the relationships. The wizard has made every effort for your new database to create a complex, functional network of tables and to link them together. If you have worked through the previous chapter carefully, you will not have any difficulty reconstructing this 'relationships box':

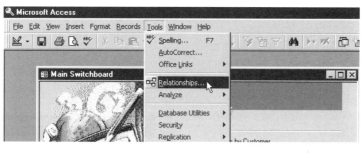

Choose the menu command TOOLS/RELATIONSHIPS.

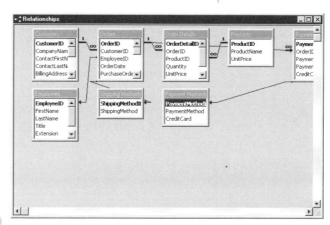

The Relationships window is displayed. Drag some tables with the cursor on the title bar …

289

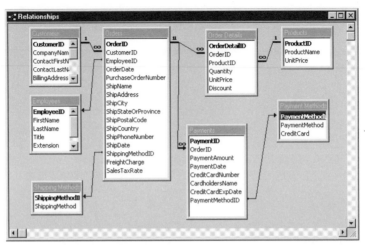

3 ... and arrange the separate lists so that all the relationships are visible.

4 Save the new layout straight away.

The relationship line between two tables shows you what kind of relationship it is. If the line is thicker at the ends, then it is a relationship with referential integrity. In other words, this relationship prevents data that are still linked with other tables from being deleted. These relationships also show the relationship type (standard 1:n), the 1 representing the field that may occur once, while the algebra stands for n records (e.g. a clear-cut customer number in the customer table which can occur n times in the order table).

Entering orders

The acquisition of order data is managed by a form that you can retrieve simply by selecting the first option on the switchboard.

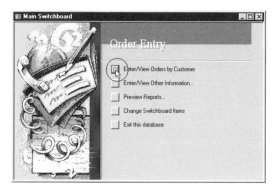

1 Click the first option on the switchboard.

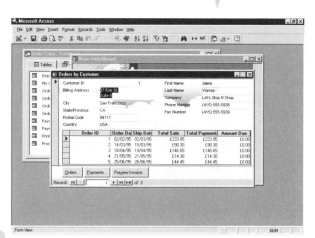

2 The form is opened, and you can display the individual customers, using the record navigator, ...

291

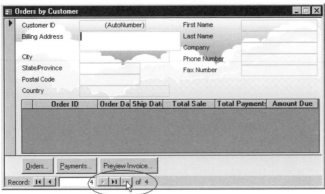

3 ... or enter new
customers.

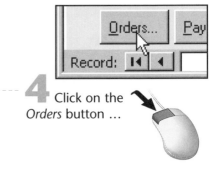

4 Click on the
Orders button ...

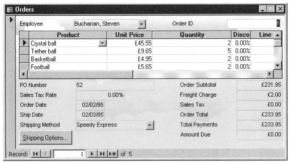

5 ... and open the subform in which the
individual orders can be processed. Enter
additional records for the customers displayed
or change the order data already acquired.

The *Payments* button leads to another
linked form, which shows the terms of payment
for the customer.

How do we create buttons like this? The drawing of the objects is
easy enough, but for the link to the table data you must turn to
module programming. This is because buttons start modules, which
are programs written in Visual Basic and stored under the *Modules*
tab in the database window. Have a look at which module is
concealed behind a button:

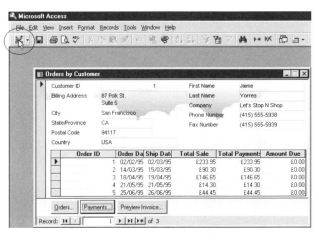

When the order form is displayed
switch to design mode.

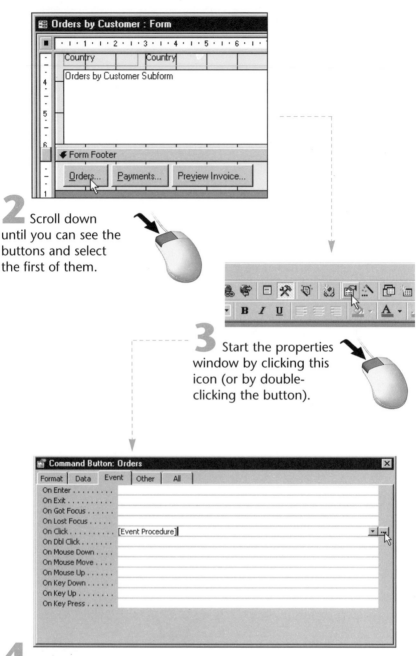

2 Scroll down until you can see the buttons and select the first of them.

3 Start the properties window by clicking this icon (or by double-clicking the button).

4 On this tab you will find the event properties and our button starts a procedure, *On Click*, as you can see.

```
Form_Orders by Customer : Class Module                      _ □ ×
Orders                         ▼   Click                              ▼
    Private Sub Orders_Click()                                        ▲
    On Error GoTo Err_Orders_Click
        If IsNull(Me![CustomerID]) Then
            MsgBox "Enter customer information before entering orde
        Else
            DoCmd.DoMenuItem acFormBar, acRecordsMenu, acSaveRecord
            DoCmd.OpenForm "Orders", , , , acEdit
        End If

    Exit_Orders_Click:
        Exit Sub

    Err_Orders_Click:
        MsgBox Err.Description
        Resume Exit_Orders_Click
    End Sub
    Private Sub Payments_Click()                                      ▼
≡≣ ◄                                                          ►
```

5 This is the VBA module with the button
procedure which is started by clicking.

Advanced users should also spend
time on this part of Access;
programming is indispensable
with complex database models.

We shall not investigate these
buttons any further, as this
would be going beyond the
scope of an introductory book.

Writing invoices

There is also provision for invoicing on the main form, even if no
separate option for it can be found. This is because the invoice can
be printed immediately on the acquisition or editing of the order,
again at the touch of a button.

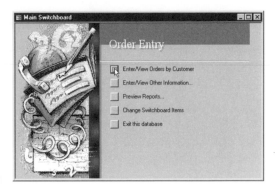

1 Again start the order form from the switchboard.

2 Scroll down to the record of the customer to whom you want to send an invoice and click on the *Preview Invoice* button.

3 Here you can enter or change the standard invoice data, and by clicking OK ...

4 ... the invoice is printed in the form of a report.

5 Look at the report design.

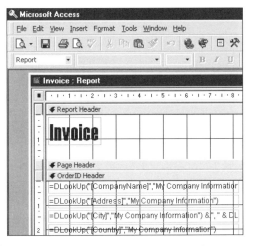

6 Grouping is by order number, and the recipient information is kept in the grouping section.

297

	ID	Product Name				Quantity		Unit Price

◆ Detail

	ProductID	ProductName			Quantity		UnitPrice	

◆ OrderID Footer

7 The actual invoice data can be found in the detail section ...

		Subtotal		=Sum(CLng([Qua
		Freight Charge		FreightCharge
		Sales Tax		=CLng([SalesTax
		Order Total		=[Subtotal]+[Frei
		Total Payments		=IIf(IsNull([Orderl
		Total Due		=[Order Total]-nz

8 ... and the footer section contains the totals, tax and invoice amount.

The individual formulas are worth a closer look. Open the properties window of an element and take a good look at the calculations. They can be found on the last tab as control element content.

Exporting data to Excel

The Excel spreadsheet program is one of the especially useful parts of the Office package. For the user it is often not easy to decide whether Excel or Access is the better tool, and Excel is often the easier way to achieve something quickly.

But there is a clear difference between them: Excel cannot build relational links. As soon as you have several different databases to deal with (customers and orders, vehicles and parts, products and suppliers, etc.), you should go for Access.

Export your data from the Access database into an Excel table and calculate the number fields with formulas and functions – something that Access is not so good at. Follow these steps, for example, if you want to continue processing total sales in Excel to create a chart:

1 Exit from the switchboard and click the query tab in the database window.

2 Select this query …

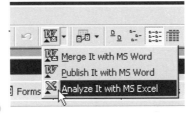

3 … and transfer the result of the query into an Excel table.

299

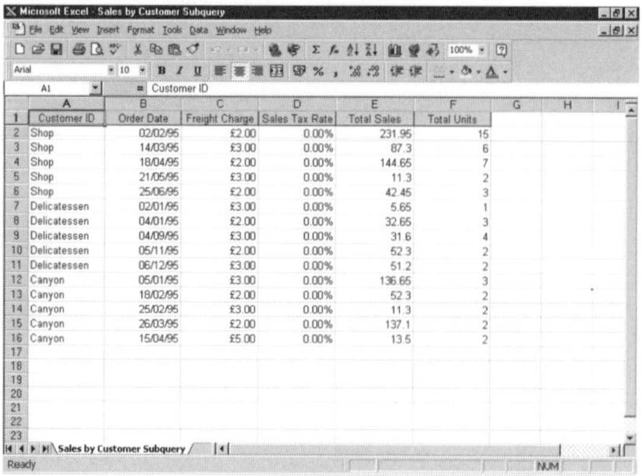

	Customer ID	Order Date	Freight Charge	Sales Tax Rate	Total Sales	Total Units
2	Shop	02/02/95	£2.00	0.00%	231.95	15
3	Shop	14/03/95	£3.00	0.00%	87.3	6
4	Shop	18/04/95	£2.00	0.00%	144.65	7
5	Shop	21/05/95	£3.00	0.00%	11.3	2
6	Shop	25/06/95	£2.00	0.00%	42.45	3
7	Delicatessen	02/01/95	£3.00	0.00%	5.65	1
8	Delicatessen	04/01/95	£2.00	0.00%	32.65	3
9	Delicatessen	04/09/95	£3.00	0.00%	31.6	4
10	Delicatessen	05/11/95	£2.00	0.00%	52.3	2
11	Delicatessen	06/12/95	£3.00	0.00%	51.2	2
12	Canyon	05/01/95	£3.00	0.00%	136.65	3
13	Canyon	18/02/95	£2.00	0.00%	52.3	2
14	Canyon	25/02/95	£3.00	0.00%	11.3	2
15	Canyon	26/03/95	£2.00	0.00%	137.1	2
16	Canyon	15/04/95	£5.00	0.00%	13.5	2

4 The table will immediately be opened in the Excel window. You can now start to calculate or create a chart at once.

If Excel as a program is not already open, this data export opens it automatically. The worksheet opened in the process is immediately saved on the hard disk as an XLS file.

> **TIP**
> You can export both tables and queries to Excel. From the menu command FILE/SAVE AS/EXPORT you will also have the option of exporting data to Excel or in a different data format.

Experienced Excel users also know the reverse method, that is data import, started from Excel, which retrieves data from an Access database to go into an Excel table. The advantage of this method is that you can link the data dynamically, in other words, import it so that any change in the Access database is automatically reflected in the Excel table.

Data import in Excel is effected by means of the menu command DATA/EXTERNAL DATA/CREATE QUERY. These queries are processed by MS Query, which is very similar to the query module in Access.

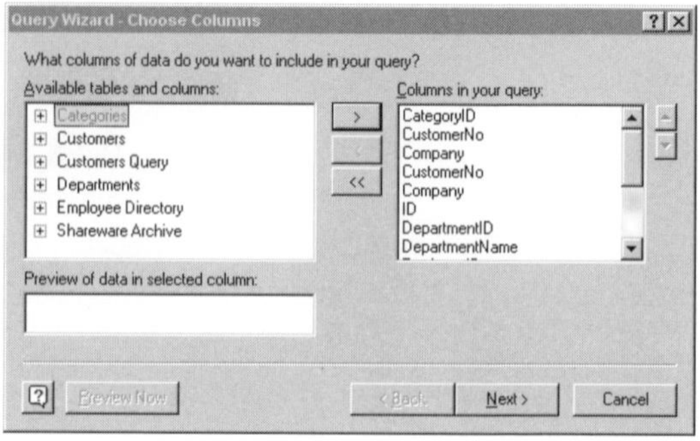

Creating Word form print files

The Word word-processing program has a form print function which you can use to send a text document to several different addressees. Whether you intend to write publicity circulars to customers, send out employee information or seek offers from different companies, the data source should always consist of an Access database. Access data can be maintained and updated, which is not so easy with Word tables.

Take a practical example. The customer table from our order processing is to serve as data source for a publicity circular by your company. So you create a form letter with dynamic customer data:

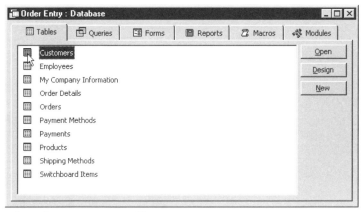

1 Select the customer table on the Tables tab of the database window.

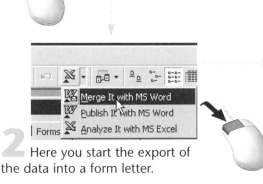

2 Here you start the export of the data into a form letter.

301

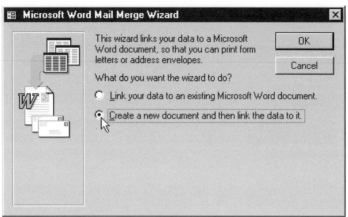

3 If you do not yet have a suitable document, one will now be created.

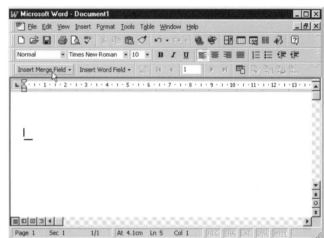

4 Word is started, the form letter is already prepared and you can insert the fields from the customer table.

5 Start with the Company field, …

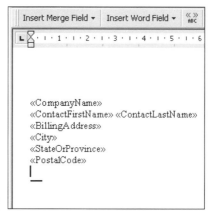

6 … and insert all the address fields one after the other. Press the ⏎ key for a new line and do not forget the blank spaces between the fields.

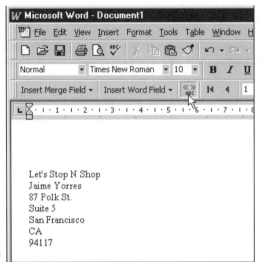

Let's Stop N Shop
Jaime Yorres
87 Polk St.
Suite 5
San Francisco
CA
94117

7 Click this button to look at the records in a preview, …

You can control and if necessary correct the link to the Access data source by way of the menu command TOOLS/FORM PRINT.

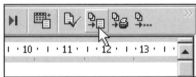

8 … click here to start the output of the form letter as a document or use the other button for printing.

Protecting databases with passwords

... which you must not forget. There is no official way of reproducing a forgotten password. If you no longer know your password, you will not be able to see the data either!

The password you have to enter to start your operating system provides generally secure protection from unauthorised access, at least if you are working with Windows NT. Windows 95 passwords do not protect data. If you are using Access to create and manage databases containing data that you don't want others using your personal computer to see, you should protect the databases themselves. Simply give them a password.

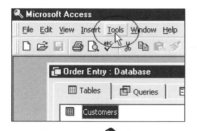

To assign a password activate the TOOLS menu ...

... and click the first menu option under SECURITY.

3 Enter a password. Confirm it by entering it a second time. Both entries will only appear as asterisks.

The password can be up to 16 characters in length. Think about upper/lower case. You can delete a password using the same menu option.

4 When you close the database and open it again, you will be asked for this password.

You will find more sophisticated protective measures by clicking on the menu command TOOLS/SECURITY. Activate the security wizard, which will take you safely through to a secure database ...

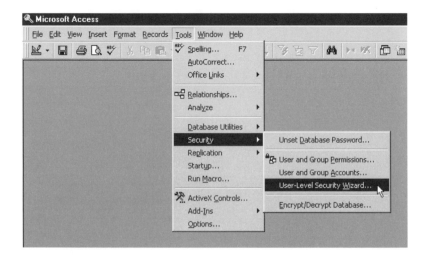

Quick progress check

Just one more time: a test of what you know. Answer the ten questions with *True* or *False* and then check the answers to see if you were right.

Question	True	False
1 There is a separate database wizard for order processing		
2 The switchboard cannot be set manually.		
3 A thicker relationship line in the Relationship window refers to referential integrity		
4 Buttons in forms usually activate a VBA module (procedure)		
5 The wizard for order processing produces invoices on forms		
6 The data for the invoice recipient is stored in the group part of the report		
7 Access is preferred to Excel when tables have to be linked		
8 An Access table cannot be used as a data source for Word form letters		
9 The database password can be as long as you like		
10 The security wizard provides comprehensive database security		

You'll find the answers in the appendix.

What's in
this chapter?

From time to time, everyone faces the problem of your program refusing to do what you want it to and responding with an incomprehensible error message. Or it fills the screen with something useless that you do not understand. What should you do?

The most important thing is to remember, everything has a reason. Almost anything the program does (almost) has an explicable cause and is recoverable. So first try to contain the error. Use the Access help functions, read the descriptions carefully and then try again. You will find some of these 'inexplicable phenomena' and 'insoluble problems', along with their solutions, in this chapter.

How do I get help quickly?

The Office Assistant

Your busy little friend is always standing by to help. He often offers his help unsolicited, but he can be deactivated at any time and recalled whenever he is needed.

1.   Click on the box with the cross in the top right of the Assistant title bar if you want to deactivate it.

2.   Open the Help menu and select MICROSOFT ACCESS HELP to activate the Office Assistant. Simply type in a question and press the ⎯ key. The Assistant will immediately display all the available options.

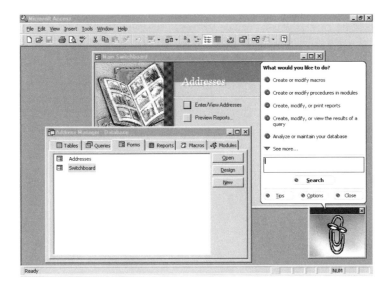

 A click on the button with the question mark in a speech bubble top right immediately activates the assistant again.

The Help Menu

You can call up the Access HELP menu at any time and read through the list of explanations. You also have an alphabetical index displayed which you can use to search for the help topic.

1   On the Help menu select the CONTENTS AND INDEX command.

2   On the *Contents* tab you will find help topics arranged into categories, while the *Index* tab displays them alphabetically by key words.

Context-sensitive help

Searching through help topics is a very time-consuming process. Often you need help for something straight away (such as a control element on the form) and for this there is context-sensitive help. This form of help focuses specifically on what you are doing or processing on screen at the time.

1   Set up the situation for which you need help.

2   Simply press the F1 key for context-sensitive help.

What's this?

Is there a menu command you don't understand? Does the icon displayed mean nothing to you? Then you should use What's this?, which gives you information about whatever you click on.

1   On the question mark menu select the WHAT'S THIS? option or the key combination ⇧ + F1.

2   Open the menu or click on the icon for which you need help.

The action assigned to the menu item or icon (e.g. save, open, print) is not performed in this case. Instead you will see a full explanation of it.

Dialog help

There is one other help facility and, although hard to find, it is very useful when dealing with dialog boxes. If you have opened a dialog field, you can display a short explanation for many of the individual options displayed in the active dialog field. For example:

1   Activate the corresponding dialog field using the menu command TOOLS/OPTIONS.

2   Place the cursor on the first option on the *View* tab.

3   Press the right mouse button and click on What's this? for an explanation of this option.

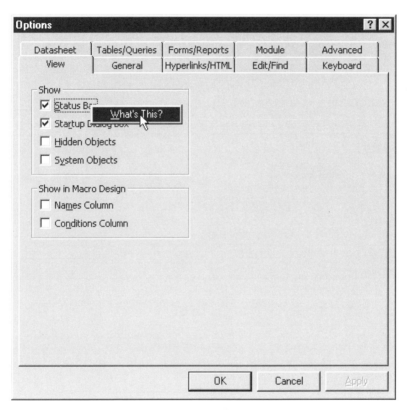

Help, I can't find my database!

If you are unable to open your database after starting Access, there are several possible causes. Often, the database file has been (inadvertently) deleted, moved or renamed. Try to locate the file on your hard disk. We shall assume that you are looking for the database called *Shareware.mdb*:

1	From the Start menu choose the FIND command and in the submenu the FILES/FOLDERS command.
2	Enter the name on the Named line. Part of the file name will suffice. If you want to find all databases, enter *.mdb.
3	Start the search by clicking on the Find Now button.

The program will now search the entire hard disk for the file or files and display the locations in the search window. Look at the second column, which shows you which folder contains your database.

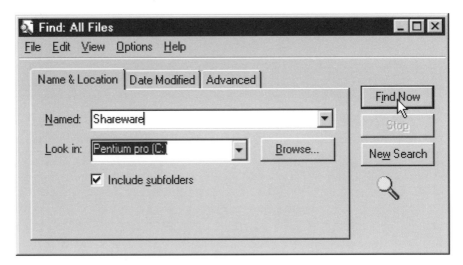

Help, my table is on strike!

All kinds of minor and not so minor problems can crop up when working with tables in Table Design or in Tables View. Here is a list of such problems and their solutions:

Problem	Solution
The column is not wide enough for the data.	You can make any column wider by dragging the right side of the column selector at the top of the column to the right. A double-click will widen the column to its optimum width.

Problem	Solution
I can only enter a limited number of characters.	The field length has probably turned out not to be big enough. Switch to table design mode and in field properties change the first setting (field size) for this field.
The column should really be called something else.	No problem. Select the menu command FORMAT/RENAME COLUMN. Enter a different column name. This will at the same time be the new field name in the table structure.
I cannot enter anything in a column, I just keep hearing a sound.	Look at the status bar, which shows you when you are trying to make an entry in an AutoNumber field. You cannot enter values in fields with this file type; the value is incremented automatically.
The entry in a field is not accepted. How do I get out again?	If you have made an incorrect entry (e.g. text in a number field), the record is nonetheless selected as 'Changed'. Press the Esc key to exit the field.
I want to restore a deleted record, but the UNDO option on the EDIT menu is not active.	This option will rarely be active in data acquisition or modification because all the changes are immediately written to the database. This also means that deleted records are irretrievably lost.
I always have to enter a telephone number in a certain format for the entry to be accepted. How can I get round this?	Switch to table design mode. If you place the cursor in the field with the telephone number, you will see an entry mask, which you can delete at any time, at the bottom in field properties under *Format*.
A field in my table contains a list of suggestions. I would like to enter my own contents but it won't let me.	The field was created by the Lookup Wizard and it is probably getting the data from another table. Open the table in design mode and activate the wizard again. It also provides an option by which you can enter data yourself.

313

Help, my form won't do what I want it to!

Forms are the best helpers in data acquisition, but only as long as they work. A faulty form can be very time-consuming and annoying. But you may be able to spare yourself this if you read the following:

Problem

When I press the ⬅ key in a particular field, the selection jumps to the wrong field.

Solution

The tab order is incorrect. Switch to the form's design mode and select the menu command VIEW/TAB ORDER. Drag the field that is out of sequence to the desired position with the mouse pointer in the grey box on the left side.

My form is much longer than it should be. As a result, you cannot see all the fields can be seen together, and there is a large blank space at the bottom.

This is the form footer. Mask out the section that is not generally used. To do this, open the form in design mode and drag the bottom line of the form upwards until the *Form Footer* section is closed.

My form contains fields on a second page, even though there is enough room on the first page. How can I prevent this annoying scrolling?

You must arrange the fields appropriately in form design. Also, check whether or not a page break has been inserted. This is a small dotted line on the left side of the design window.

A form from my form module displays no data. What's happened?

Check which table or query the form is connected to. For this, switch to design mode and double-click top left in the corner in which the two rulers meet, on the field with the small black square. In the Properties window check the data origin. If the table or query displayed here supplies no data, then the form will be empty too.

Problem	Solution
I cannot enter anything in the first field with the data type *AutoNumber*. How can I bar this form element so that it is not selected?	Select the control element in design mode and open the Properties window. On the second tab *Data* you will find the properties *Enabled* and *Locked*. Set the first one to *No* and the second to *Yes*.
Dates in forms are always shown in the shortest format. Can this display be expanded so that the month for example is written out in full?	Yes it can, and again in design mode. Open the Properties of the control element and select the line *Entry Format*. If you click on the icon to the right of the line, you will activate a wizard that will show you how to add an expanded date format to the element.
When I create a combination field, the wizard is no longer activated. What's happened?	You have inadvertently deactivated the icon at the very top right of the toolbox. This is how the wizard is activated.

Help, my query is not working!

The query as a basis for forms or reports brings together data from different tables. Take special care with the correctness of the relationships and do not use any fields that do not exist.

Problem	Solution
My query covers two tables with 20 records each. If I execute the query, I get 400 records as a result. What's wrong?	The two tables are not linked together. If there is more than one table in the query window, there must be a relationship line from the primary key field of one table to a number field of the other.
Right at the beginning I forgot to insert a table. Can I rectify this?	Select the menu command QUERY/DISPLAY TABLE. Now you can add further table windows. If you no longer need a window, delete it with the Delete key.
My query does not show me some of the fields, although they are listed in the query window.	Check that there is a check mark in the respective field on the *Show* line.

Problem	Solution
I want to sort the query result by several fields. Which field will be sorted first?	The field that is on the extreme left in query design.
How can I sort the query by a field that is not displayed?	Drag the field name right across to the left into the first column and remove the check mark on the line *Show*.
I want to enter the result of a query in a new table. How do I do that?	On the QUERY Menu select the command MAKE-TABLE QUERY. This is how you generate a new table.
When I start my query I always have a dialog field displayed in which I am asked for a field that is unknown to me. What's wrong?	You have used a field name in a column that does not/has ceased to exist. You may have previously deleted the field from the table structure or it is a simple typing error.
Why does the query result end up basically empty?	In practice the criteria on the Criteria line are usually incorrect. Limit the problem by retrieving each field into the query individually, entering criteria and executing the query.

Help, my report is not displaying what it should!

Even more elaborate than form design is report design. The many sections are not easy to handle and you will need a lot of time to produce the first really useful reports.

Problem	Solution
My report displays all the captions but does not supply any records.	Look at the data origin. If you click on the box top left with the small black square in report design, you can see in the Properties field which table or query is supplying the data.

Problem	Solution
The line spacings in my report are far too big.	Open the report design and look at the detail section. If you bring the top line of the next section quite close to the control elements, the spacing will become less. You may have to first select the elements by clicking to the left on the outside and moving to the top.
How can I delete a grouping element that I no longer need?	When you select the menu command VIEW/ SORTING AND GROUPING all the grouping fields are displayed. Select the line with the field and switch it to *No* under *Group Header*. This removes this grouping from the report.
My report does not fit on one page in the horizontal. What can I do? Do I have to make all the control elements smaller individually?	No, first select the menu command FILE/PAGE SETUP and find out whether you can get it to fit by reducing the size of the page margins or adjusting the column widths.
When I want to make a report column smaller I first edit the caption in the page header, then the element in the detail section. Isn't there a quicker way?	Yes there is. You can simply drag a frame with the mouse around the two elements to select them. If you now reduce the size of an element, the effect is the same on the other element.
How can I print out the report data on a form where the report header and footer have already been printed?	Choose the menu command FILE/PAGE SETUP. On the first tab *Margins* you will find an option *Print data only*.

317

This appendix contains the answers to the progress indicators at the end of each chapter.

Chapter 1

The abbreviation DBMS stands for **Database Management System** (1). It refers to the software used to manage a database.

Databases consist of **tables** (2), forms, **queries** (3), reports, macros and modules.

The core of a database consists of tables that are linked together. We call a database with links **relational** (4).

Each column in a table is called a **field** (5), the column heading is also the field name. The **field property** (6) is changed to predefine the field size or the contents.

You can start Access either by way of the **Start menu** (7) or the shortcut bar.

An Access database is stored in a file with the extension **MDB** (8); the file can be as big as **1 gigabyte** (9).

You set the standard database directory by way of the menu command **Tools/Options** (10).

In the example database *Northwind.mdb* tables are linked; the relationships can be viewed by way of the menu command **Tools/Relationships** (11).

The database window contains **six** (12) modules. An object (such as a table) can be viewed in design mode by pressing the **Design** (13) button. Top left on the toolbar there is a button you can click to switch straight to **Datasheet view** (14).

Chapter 2

1. False, of course. You can create as many tables as you like. Only the size of the computer's memory would limit the number.

2. True. MDB stands for *Microsoft Database.*

3. False. Up to 64 characters are allowed, including numbers and some special characters.

4. False. The choice of field data types available in table design is limited to nine.

5. False. The primary key goes to the field in the table that is clear-cut.

6. False. It is true only if the last field is selected. Otherwise the ⟵ key switches to the next field.

7. True. This is how you open an entry field quickly.

8. False. The pencil shows that the record is being processed and has not yet been saved.

9. True. With it you can jump forwards and back to a record or to the first and last record.

10. False. You can also enter numbers, but they are then treated as text. The numbers are not therefore suitable for calculation purposes.

11. False. You have the option of ascending or descending sorts. The buttons are located next to one another.

12. True. The highlighting determines the filtering.

13. False. When the table is closed all the filters are reset.

14. False. You should create all numbers that can be combined with characters and special characters as text fields.

15. True. You can click on the entry with the mouse and this will take you straight to the Internet address.

Chapter 3

1a The wizard is made available immediately after the start (or by way of the menu command FILE/NEW).

2c The style determines the background, the font and the font size of all forms.

3a Wizards always produce (virtually) complete databases.

4b You use validity rules to control what the user is allowed to do.

5b Forms clear the view of tables or queries.

6c Entry fields, text in the form are called control elements.

7a Like the form the report also displays table data.

8b This formula is always used if today's date is used.

9b You will also find the switchboard as a form in the forms module.

10a The boxes control window size and display.

Chapter 4

To set up a new database in the Access window, open the **File** (1) menu. You can only have **one** (2) database open at any time: any database already open will be closed when you open or set up a new one. The records have already been saved; they are saved at the time of **acquisition** (3). The memo field can hold up to **32,000** (4) characters; unlike a text field, this is used for remarks and explanations. To see the links between the different tables, look under **Relationships** (5) in the **Tools** (6) menu. Forms are divided into sections. The heading is usually in the **Header section** (7), the data in the **Detail section** (8). To select more than one control element of the form, use the **mouse** (9) to draw a box around the elements concerned. The elements **need not** (10) be enclosed in the box. To call up an element property, **double-** (11) click on the element or the *Properties* icon. Which table the form is linked to is shown by the **Record origin** (12) property. Reports are found in the **Reports module** (13) of the database window. Double-clicking on a report opens it in **Page View** (14). The cursor now looks like a magnifying glass, and clicking it on the report **reduces** (15) it to page view. Reports are also divided into sections: the heading is in the **Header section** (16), the data in the **Detail section** (17). Page numbers are always found in the **Page footer** (18).

Chapter 5

1. True, in the Windows 95 and Windows NT environments.

2. False. It introduces the path indication to a folder.

3. False. You can choose all the fields individually.

4. True. Each field can be redefined.

5. True. The primary key is vital.

6. False, the primary key field must be of the *AutoNumber* type.

7. False. Select the menu command TOOLS/RELATIONSHIPS and see for yourself.

8. False. The line must be double-clicked.

9. True. The database is consequently more secure.

10. True. These control elements list the records from other tables.

Chapter 6

1C   There is the OLE object type for pictures.

2B   On the left-hand side in form design.

3H   The sequence becomes apparent when you enter data.

4I   Queries collect the fields from different tables.

5E   Adds tables or field lists of tables.

6J   Ascending or descending sorts are possible.

7G   Criteria can be extremely varied.

8D   In addition to As we also have Between, Not, And and Or.

9A   Function key F2 on its own simply opens the field.

10F   Also an option on the Query Menu: Parameters.

Chapter 7

1b   All database objects can be copied by way of the clipboard.

2c   The line is created as soon as you release the mouse.

3a   The report needs a data basis.

4b   The style provides for the correct font.

5b   The title belongs in the header.

6c   The row is selected by a click at the side.

7a   The page number (= Page) is repeated on every page.

8b   The box lists groups and sorts.

9a   Font, colours and lines of the selected section are changed.

10b   Many Avery labels are available for selection.

Chapter 8

The fields in a table structure that are linked to fields in other tables must be of the **Number** (1) field data type. The size of these fields is given by **Long Integer** (2). Relationships between the tables can be viewed and changed under Tools/**Relationships** (3). To create a relationship the **Primary key field** (4) of one table is dragged to the linked field of the other table. You can delete a selected relationship line with the **Delete** (5) key. You can justify form elements by way of the **Format** (6) menu. You can increase the vertical spacing with the **Align** (7) option from this menu. A subform makes the data from a **different** (8) table or query available for editing. If there is a subform in the main form, **two** (9) different navigation buttons can be seen. The outer arrows control the records in the **main form** (10).

Chapter 9

1. True. You will find it after starting under *New Database* or under FILE/NEW.

2. False. The switchboard can be found under TOOLS/STARTUP.

3. True. The relationship type is also displayed (usually 1:n).

4. True. The procedure can be found in the module sheet, the link with the button in its properties.

5. False. Invoices are always created as reports.

6. True. The group also contains the customer address.

7. True. Excel is better for calculations in two-dimensional tables.

8. False. Access is the ideal supplier for form letter data.

9. False. You only have 16 characters available.

10. True. You can also divide users into groups, create user accounts and manage database access as far as object level.

Assistant/Wizard There are two kinds of assistant/wizard. The Office Assistant is the funny paper clip in a small window who occasionally offers help or, if active, issues messages. The Access wizards are programs that can be activated for the creation of a table, a form, a query or a report. They guide the user through the process interactively.

AutoNumber The field type that ensures that a number is automatically incremented in the field when a new record is created. AutoNumber fields cannot be written by the user.

ClipArt This is what we call graphics created on the computer and stored on the computer.

Combination field These are the control elements that when clicked offer a list of data (also called drop-down fields). Combination fields only appear in forms. They are either created by wizards or entered directly by way of the combo box tool from the toolbox. The origin of the data is decided by the element *property Record* origin.

Command button Drawn elements on forms which, as a property, have a link to a VBA program or a macro and activate it when they are clicked while you are working on a form. Command buttons are marked with a tool from the toolbox.

Control element This is a field in a form or report. Control elements have properties that are assigned and processed in design mode.

Criteria In queries, individual fields can be provided with criteria. To do this we enter the criterion on the line of the same name, and the data that are the output of the query are filtered according to this criterion.

Cursor The special character that flashes in an entry field when you click the field with the mouse. You can move the cursor in this field with the cursor keys.

Database The collection of objects (tables, queries, forms, reports, macros and modules) for the storage and editing of data. Access is a program for the processing of databases.

Database window The first and most important window in a database, which shows the individual objects divided into modules. To switch to a different module, simply click the appropriate tab. The database window can be activated by way of the WINDOW menu.

Data type See **Field data type**

Date Access gets the date from the operating system, which, in turn, obtains it from a battery-operated computer clock. To insert the date in fields, forms or reports there are a number of date functions (=Date(), =Month(), etc.). You will find a list of the functions in the Editor window.

Design view It is in this view that the structure of a table (with field list) is processed. In this view you can see how the fields and other elements (text, lines, graphics) are arranged in a form or report. There is a button top left for switching to design view.

Editor This is an entry window that can be opened when processing the field properties of table fields, forms or report fields. Click on the small button

325

with three dots to the right of the selected properties field. The Editor offers all the formulas and functions that can be entered in this field.

Exclusive mode Databases can in principle be processed by several users at the same time, except where you have opened them in exclusive mode. To do this, after *File/Open* Database, check the box labelled 'Exclusive' and then access will be barred to every other user on the network.

Field This is what we call a column in a table or the element on a form or report that is filled with data on display (form) or output (report). Table fields have field properties; form/report fields have control element properties.

Field data type The producer of a database uses this to determine what type of data may be entered in the field. If the field is of the text type, the user has a choice of entering text, numbers and special characters. Number fields may only contain numbers, date fields only dates, etc. A special type is AutoNumber; this field automatically fills itself with the next higher number.

Field name Fields must have a name in table design, which then serves as a column heading when the table is displayed. The field name is less important in the form or report; it can be determined by way of the control element properties.

File name The name for a dataset (file) stored on the data carrier. File names can be up to 256 characters in length, including spaces and some special characters. Added to the end of the file name and separated by a dot, is the file extension (e.g. MDB for Access databases). If you cannot see these extensions, activate them in Windows Explorer under *View/Options*.

Filter With a filter you ensure that only a certain subset of the data that a table or a query contains appears as output. Filters are temporarily activated in the table sheet, in the datasheet or in form mode, but lose their effect when the object is closed. To use filters permanently, they are set in queries and saved with the queries.

Formula A mathematical expression for the calculation of data, which generally, in addition to operators (+, −, etc.) and logic characters (> greater than, < less than, etc.), incorporates the fields of a table. Field names are then written in square brackets (e.g. *[Quantity]*[Price]*). Formulas can be used in the table structure, in queries and in form/report design.

Function This is a mathematical calculation that is provided by the program. The function SUM(*[field name]*) calculates the sum of all the contents of *field name*. Functions are used in queries and in form/report design. A list of all the functions can be found in the Editor, which is activated by the icon with the three dots to the right of a field being processed.

Header/footer section Forms and reports are divided into sections and the heading usually appears in the header section. The footer section contains page numbers and other elements. In reports there is the distinction between report header/footer and page header/footer.

Home page This is the internet presence of a company or a private individual. When you call

an internet address, you usually see the home page. Access can store such home page calls in records with a separate data type (hyperlink).

HTML The language of the internet. Home pages are programmed in HTML.

Hyperlink This is the link in a record that refers to an internet address. Hyperlinks can also be used in forms and reports to switch from one object to another. Other programs such as Excel or Word can even be activated with hyperlinks.

Import/Export To incorporate data from 'outside', i.e. from other files, into the database, it is imported. There is the option of creating a dynamic link, where the original data remains in its place, or of inserting the data completely. Data is exported when it is needed in a different database, a different file format. Access tables can, for example, be exported as Excel tables.

Link See **Relationship**

Macro This is a sequence of actions performed in the Access program. Access macros are small programs that open and close objects, issue messages and select or process records. Macros are the time-saving alternative to VBA procedures, although they are not as flexible as the latter.

Module The name of a tab in the database window (tables tab, queries tab, forms tab, etc.), or a program sheet with VBA procedures, stored on the last tab *Module*.

Navigation This means movement in tables, scrolling between records and the selection of certain records. The table sheet or datasheet and the form provide arrow buttons in the record navigator (bottom left of the window) for navigation.

Object A table, a form and a query are objects, likewise a report or a macro/module sheet. The database window manages all the objects of a database.

OLE Abbreviation for *Object Linking and Embedding*. The term stands for a method for the insertion of parts of other, external programs into an Access window. If a record contains a picture, for example, a field with the data type OLE

object must be provided for it. If the record is then acquired, the name of the OLE object (the file name of the picture) can appear in this field.

Option A choice offered by the program. If you open a menu, for example, you can choose one of the menu options. If you start a dialog, (e.g. with *Tools/Options*), numerous options are displayed on each tab for selection/deselection.

Parameter query A parameter is the additional information required to execute a query. The parameter query needs this before it collects and presents the data from the tables concerned with the query. To effect a parameter query, the question is simply written in square brackets on the criteria line of the respective field.

Password In addition to the user password that you have to enter as a Windows 95/NT user, to gain access to the operating system, the database can also be password-protected. This makes it encrypted, so the file can only be opened by entering the right password. The password is assigned by using *Tools/Security*.

Primary key The field in the table structure that clearly identifies each individual record. The content of the field must not recur in any other field. Only then can links between tables be guaranteed to work. If no primary key field can be found when a table is newly created, Access creates it automatically.

Printing You can print the object currently being processed on the screen by choosing printer button or with *File/Print*. Access takes over the system printer made available by Windows, but cannot offer any printer installation of its own. However, different settings (number of copies, etc.) can be made before printing under *File/Print*.

Procedure This is a program that has been written in VBA (Visual Basic for Applications) and saved in a module sheet. Procedures are assigned to the properties of control elements or command buttons in forms.

Property Every element in a form or report and every table field has its list of properties. In form/report fields they are displayed in a separate window after double-clicking or by clicking the properties icon. Table field properties are displayed in the bottom half of the design window.

Query An agreement about which fields from individual tables are displayed, optionally also with an indication of the sorting and criteria that must be satisfied for this purpose. Queries are saved and each time they are retrieved they show the present data from the tables. Queries do not store any data themselves.

Record A row in a table is called a record. The content of the fields displayed in a form is also a record, likewise the output of a line in the detail section of a report.

Record marker When a record in a form, datasheet or table is being processed, the record marker to the left of the line or form edge indicates the status. A pencil shows that the last change has not been saved, while the black triangle refers to saved records.

Referential integrity This is how Access monitors the relationships between tables and ensures that no data is lost. If you try to delete data in a table that is referred to by another table, the referential integrity will stop you doing so.

Relationship Tables maintain a relationship if they are linked by common fields. If the supplier number in an item table is linked to the supplier number in the supplier table, then these two tables are in a relationship with one another.

Report The report is used to arrange and save the type of output of fields on the printer. A saved report does not itself contain any data, just the arrangement of the data. The data from the table or query are only inserted on output in page view or on the printer.

Selection-based filter A filter that raises the present selection to a criterion. If, for example, an entry 'London' in the 'Location' field is selected when this filter is retrieved, only records with this entry in this field are displayed.

Sorting Tables can be sorted by individual columns (fields). Simply select the column and activate the sort icon. Ascending sorts arrange the special characters and numbers first, then the text alphabetically from A to Z.

Tabs The database window arranges its modules in tabs. Many of the dialogs, as under *Tools/Options*, have their numerous options arranged on tabs.

Tab order Determines the order in which the fields of a form are selected when it is opened for the acquisition or editing of table data. If the wrong field is selected after pressing the ⏎ key, you must change the tab order (VIEW menu).

Toolbar When a database is retrieved, the database toolbar can be found at the top of the program window (under the menu bar). This bar changes its tool layout according to the object being processed at the time. Many tools can only be activated when a corresponding element has been selected. For example, you can only use the bold tool when a control element has been selected that can be made bold (name or text field).

VBA Abbreviation for Visual Basic for Applications, the programming language that has now become standard for the Office product family. VBA programs (procedures) are

created and maintained in
module sheets in the last
module in the database
window, and are activated by
command buttons or by way of
the properties of control
elements. There are also
automatic procedures that
control a database without any
action on the part of the user.
VBA programming is real object-
oriented programming.

Word The word processing
program of the Office product
family with a direct interface to
Access tables. They can, for
instance, be transferred as
Word-form print source. Access
data can also be exported as
text files in Word format.

Zoom window Activated by
[⇧] + [F2] , it displays the
content of the field in which the
cursor is located or which has
been selected at the time in a
large dialog field. Zoom
windows facilitate the creation
and the editing of complex
formulas in query columns, in
control elements or in the table
structure.

Index

A

B

C

categories 158
  linked 152
changing 60, 91 et seq.
  Database Wizard 80
changing table layout 67
clicking, mouse 15
ClipArt 325
closing 41, 59
colours 236
column header 199
column heading 65
column limitation 175
column width, optimum 69, 175
column, masking out 68 et seq.,
  207
  inverting 199
  reducing 67
  several 69
  sorting line 206
  superimposing 68 et seq.
  widening 57 et seq.
  wider 58
combination field 170, 192, 266
  creating 172 et seq.
combination field tool 265
command button 325
company logo 87
configuration of the field names 60
confirming entry 58
connecting line 223, 262
context-sensitive help 310
control element content 241
control elements 330
  deleting 103 et seq.
Corel Draw 186
creating buttons 293
  modules 293
creating database tables 220
creating a subform 276 et seq.

breakdown 277
  layout 278
creating tables 51 et seq., 260
  field size 53
criteria 209, 211, 329
criteria line 210, 215
  characters 211
  operators 211
currency 66
cursor 325
customer numbers the same 56
customer table 257

D

data acquisition 130, 166
  forms 120
data entry format 97
data export, VBA 37
data exporting 299 et seq.
  form 166, 189
  sorting 70
  validity rule 94
data import into Excel 300
  VBA 37
data loss 60
data origin 133
data redundancy 258
data source 232
data type 41, 50, 66, 123, 327
  hyperlink 66
  memo 124
  text 53
  list 66
data type 326
  AutoNumber 152, 186
  changing 60
data type list 268
database 18, 325
  creating 47 et seq., 80 et seq.,
    116 et seq., 144 et seq., 284

333

function 328
function keys 12

G

greetings card 91
group 72
group fields 140
grouping 140, 243, 297
grouping field 233
grouping levels 242

H

hard disk 25
header section 329
help 308 et seq.
  database 311
  dialog 310
  form 314
  menu 310
  Office Assistant 309
  query 315
  report 316
  table 312
  What's this? 310
help functions 308
help menu 310
holiday bookings 267
holiday offers 254
home page 61, 328
  saving call in records 328
HOW 211
HTML 328
hyperlink 61, 67, 328

I

icon 21
ID field 152

importing 328
in folders 24
in tables 60
  arrow buttons 60
in the background 232
  reducing to icon size 288
integrity, referential 162, 330
internet 61
invoice 282
  writing 295
invoicing 284
item data 33
item database 19
items 46

K

key 19
key fields 287
  for links 287
key symbol 186
keyboard 10 et seq.

L

label format 247
label size 248
Labels Wizard 247
labels 246
  arranging 248
landscape format 235
last record 60
layout window 235
layout, form 191
line selecting 93, 240
link 331
  key fields 287
  relational 163, 223
linking 38
  moving 38

T

tab order 324
table categories 148
  business 148
  personal 148
table design, field data types
    66 et seq.
  saving 54 et seq., 65
table field format 97
Tables Wizard 146 et seq.,
    182 et seq.
  categories 148
tables 18, 56
  adding 201
  copying from database 222
  deleting 205
  filtering 72
  in Excel 299
  opening 40, 56
  pasting 201, 205
  acquiring data 56 et seq.
  changing layout 67
  navigating 60
  viewing relationships 126
tables list 202
tables model 256
tables module 40
tables structure 91
tabs 330
task 22
task bar 22, 24
telephone numbers 52
telephone numbers fields 97
text 66
text field 52
title element 239
title for form 129
toolbar 330
toolbox 130, 170, 243
  activating 266

Tools/Relationships 159, 261
Tools/Security 306
Tools/Start 288
travel agency 256

U

user name 21
user password 328

V

validity check 94
validity message 97
validity rule 94 et seq.
VBA 37, 330 et seq.
  development environment 37
VBA module 295
VBA programs 37
video 186
viewing 126 et seq.
views 42
Visual Basic 37, 293
Visual Basic for Applications 37,
    330

W

What's this? 310
Windows 145
Windows Explorer 25
windows, arranging 126
  closing 35
  dragging 160
  enlarging 38, 160
  sorting and grouping 243
Word 20, 301, 331
Word form print file 301
  Access data source 304
work folder 29

X

XLS file 300

Y

yes/no 67
yes/no field 126

Z

zoom factor 237
zoom tools 237
  zoom field 237
  zoom magnifying glass 237
zoom window 212, 242, 298, 331
zooming 136